Group's

BODY-BUILDING

GUIDE TO | OUTREACH

stretching out to your community

Loveland, Colorado
www.group.com

Group resources actually work!

This Group resource helps you focus on **"The 1 Thing®"**—a life-changing relationship with Jesus Christ. "The 1 Thing" incorporates our **R.E.A.L.** approach to ministry. It reinforces a growing friendship with Jesus, encourages long-term learning, and results in life transformation, because it's:

Relational
Learner-to-learner interaction enhances learning and builds Christian friendships.

Experiential
What learners experience through discussion and action sticks with them up to 9 times longer than what they simply hear or read.

Applicable
The aim of Christian education is to equip learners to be both hearers and doers of God's Word.

Learner-based
Learners understand and retain more when the learning process takes into consideration how they learn best.

Group

GROUP'S BODY-BUILDING GUIDE TO OUTREACH: STRETCHING OUT TO YOUR COMMUNITY
Copyright © 2006 Group Publishing, Inc.

The publisher thanks Embrace Teachers Omaha for allowing its handbook to be made available to the reader through Group Publishing's Web site, www.group.com. The publisher also thanks Stacey Simpson Duke for permission to publish an excerpt from her sermon "Perfect Foolishness." Finally, the publisher thanks the deputy chief of the El Paso, Texas, Fire Department for permission to use the photo on page 57.

Visit our Web site: **www.group.com**

CREDITS
Writers: Candace McMahan and Jan Kershner
Editor: Candace McMahan
Chief Creative Officer: Joani Schultz
Copy Editor: Janis Sampson
Art Director: Joey Rusk
Print Production Artist: Julia Martin
Cover Art Director and Designer: Jeff A. Storm
Cover Photographer: Rodney Stewart
Cover Design: Veronica Lucas
Production Manager: DeAnne Lear

Unless otherwise noted, Scripture taken from the HOLY BIBLE, NEW INTERNATIONAL VERSION®. Copyright © 1973, 1978, 1984 by International Bible Society. Used by permission of Zondervan Publishing House. All rights reserved.

LIBRARY OF CONGRESS CATALOGING-IN-PUBLICATION DATA
Group's body-building guide to outreach : stretching out to your community.
   p. cm.
ISBN-13: 978-0-7644-3152-4 (pbk. : alk. paper)
1. Evangelistic work. 2. Church work. I. Group Publishing.
BV3790.G89 2006
269'.2--dc22

                                    2006012392

ISBN 0-7644-3152-8

10 9 8 7 6 5 4 3 2 1   15 14 13 12 11 10 09 08 07 06

Printed in the United States of America.

DEDICATION

"Then I heard the voice of the Lord saying, 'Whom shall I send? And who will go for us?' And I said, 'Here am I. Send me!' "

—Isaiah 6:8

To all of the people who have eagerly responded to God's call to reach out to others with the love of Jesus and who have so graciously shared their stories with us, we extend our deepest thanks. Special thanks to AnnMarie Arbo, Sara Bazemore, Jonathan Bell, Lettie Connolly, Jaimie Cogua, Linda Davis, Stacey Simpson Duke, David Erdmann, Jill Greiner, Willma Heckman, Margaret Leigh-Guthrie, Michael Kutler, Kim Lockhart, Amy Morgan, Chris Perciante, Leslie Peretti, Haley Perryman, Ed Sinke, Greg Spink, Buck Stanley, Nikki Stanley, Cathy Swirbul, K.J. Tencza, Ian Vickers, Drue Warner, Laura Warner, Nancy Wilson, and Rhonda Zehrbach.

—Group Publishing

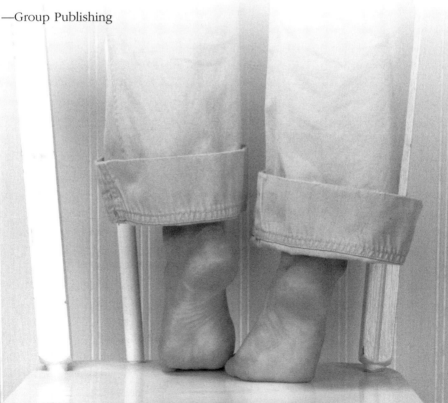

C O N T E N T S

Introduction   TOUCHED, INSPIRED, AMAZED 7

Chapter One   REACH OUT TO SINGLE MOMS 9
This church gives single moms and their
children a place of safety, equality, and favor.

Chapter Two   REACH OUT THROUGH SPORTS 21
In only four years, this church has seen
nearly 1,000 people make a faith commitment
through its sports outreach.

Chapter Three   REACH OUT TO HIGH SCHOOL STUDENTS 33
A couple of compassionate moms bring a
high school and a church together to serve
students a free lunch each week.

Chapter Four   REACH OUT TO CANCER PATIENTS 45
This church has found countless ways to
help cancer patients and their families.

Chapter Five   REACH OUT TO FIREFIGHTERS 57
A tiny, fledgling church shows how to get
involved in meaningful outreach right away,
without spending a lot of money.

Chapter Six   REACH OUT TO TEACHERS 65
A coalition of 21 churches bridges the gap
between churches and schools by encouraging
teachers throughout an entire city.

Chapter Seven   REACH OUT TO VISITORS 77
A youth group grows from 40 to over 300
by making teenage visitors feel genuinely valued.

Chapter Eight   REACH OUT TO PEOPLE WHOSE HOMES NEED REPAIR 87
A church blesses people who have
spent their lives blessing others.

C O N T E N T S

Chapter Nine   **REACH OUT TO THE HOMELESS** 95
*Churches throughout a community give homeless
families a safe haven.*

Chapter Ten   **REACH OUT TO A WHOLE COMMUNITY** 105
*This church enables people of all ages and abilities
to serve by providing accessible, just-show-up
outreach projects on the first and third Saturdays
of each month.*

Chapter Eleven   **REACH OUT TO YOUR NEIGHBORHOOD** 115
*A man and wife single-handedly build a sense
of community by reaching out to everyone in
their neighborhood.*

Chapter Twelve   **REACH OUT TO LATCHKEY KIDS** 125
*A tiny church learns that its impact can
be much greater than its size.*

Chapter Thirteen   **REACH OUT TO YOUNG READERS** 133
*This church's summer reading program has been
going strong for more than 15 years.*

Chapter Fourteen   **REACH OUT TO DEVELOPMENTALLY CHALLENGED ADULTS** . . 145
*For more than 20 years, this church has been
teaching developmentally challenged adults
about Jesus.*

Chapter Fifteen   **REACH OUT TO NURSING HOME RESIDENTS** 155
*One couple has developed a ministry just for
nursing home residents and in the process has
touched thousands of lives.*

I N T R O D U C T I O N

Prepare to be touched, inspired, and amazed. The stories in the following pages reveal so much about God—his grace, his provision, his ability to soften and expand the human heart. In these pages you will read about people who have performed remarkable deeds of kindness and compassion. You'll read about unexpected ways these acts have affected whole communities. You'll discover just what can happen when Christians are salt and light to their neighborhoods, towns, and cities.

In Chapter 12, for example, you'll read about a tiny, 20-member church—reeling from a split—that redefined itself through simple acts of kindness. In Chapter 6, you'll read about a coalition of churches that decided to touch the lives of as many public schoolteachers as possible in their city of 400,000. In Chapter 8, you'll meet a woman who, armed with a budget of only $1,000, marshaled her congregation and community to renovate two homes of deserving people. They got the job done—and came in $300 under budget.

In telling these stories, we've learned that acts of service don't require generous budgets or large congregations; they require generous spirits and large hearts. At the same time, we've become convinced that God has planted a desire to serve in the heart of every Christian. We've discovered that Christians are longing to reach out to their neighbors, but most of them simply don't know how. We've also learned that once Christians begin to serve, they want to do more.

These stories reveal countless practical ways Christians *can* serve, ways that appeal to introverts, extroverts, the young, the old, and everyone in between. Ways that tap into each person's unique wiring so that reaching out to others becomes a source of fulfillment and joy. Whether outreach is already deeply embedded in your church's DNA or it is a facet of the Christian life your church is just beginning to explore, this book will help you find many ways to tap into your congregation's desire to serve.

Group's Body-Building Guide to OUTREACH presents 15 of the finest outreach ideas we've uncovered. Each chapter profiles one church and one population it has decided to serve. The chapter tells the background story, describing the events and personalities that gave rise to the idea, explaining what has worked well and what hasn't, and revealing the underlying principles that have made the idea successful.

We realize that reading about a full-blown, hugely successful outreach can be more daunting than inspiring. The more successful it is, the greater the tendency to think, "I don't know how we would even begin to tackle something like that." That's why we've devoted the second part of each chapter to practical steps for implementing a similar outreach in your own setting. We encourage you to identify at least one idea that resonates with you and your congregation and to take the first step toward implementing it. That step will lead to another and yet another, until one day your dream of reaching your community in new ways is a reality.

In hearing and compiling these stories, we've been blessed again and again by the ways God is moving in the hearts of his people. We are excited to share them with you, and we pray that they will inspire you to lead your church to all that God has called it to be in your community. May God bless you as you reach out to a wounded world that has never been in greater need of the love of Jesus.

CHAPTER ONE

REACH OUT TO SINGLE MOMS

This church gives single moms and their children a place
of safety, equality, and favor.

- ☑ APPEALS TO CHURCHED AND UNCHURCHED MOMS AND THEIR CHILDREN
- ☑ BUILDS AUTHENTIC RELATIONSHIPS
- ☑ CAN BE DONE BY ANY SIZE CHURCH

THE EVOLUTION OF THE IDEA

In 1997, Ken Wilson, senior pastor of Vineyard Church in Ann Arbor, Michigan, was looking for a way for his church to reach out to the community. He wanted to do something that wasn't already being done better by another organization, something the church could do better than a government agency, and something that required more than money—something that would engage the hearts of the people in his congregation. At about the same time, John Wimber, the founder of the Vineyard, passed away, and Ken focused his efforts on identifying an outreach that would also honor John Wimber's memory.

In a conversation with a single mom, he asked how a church could help her daughter. She responded, "By providing a support group for moms, where child care and dinner are provided, and where I can take part in adult conversation and find support from others facing the same challenges." Thus was born Moms' Night Out, a monthly dinner for single moms and their families. Ken launched this ministry in a sermon on December 7, 1997, saying, "When we tap into God's heart for single moms, we're tapping into a tender place in his heart, revealing something of his heart we could otherwise not know."

Later, Ken learned that John Wimber was himself raised by a single mom.

THE HEART OF THE MINISTRY

The outreach began small and simple, serving uncomplicated meals prepared at home by volunteers to a handful of moms and their kids. Eight years after the outreach began, the numbers have grown, and the program has become more complicated, but one thing has remained constant: Its cornerstone is loving, supportive relationships. As single moms pastor Nancy Wilson puts it, "Any material thing we can give these moms will fade, but relationships—love—won't."

THE SECOND TUESDAY OF EVERY MONTH...

At this writing, from September through May, the church serves a gourmet meal on the second Tuesday of every month to 50 to 60 moms. From 6:30 to 7:30, they eat dinner at elegantly set tables for eight. The meal has been prepared by a team of five chefs and served by an eight-member wait staff. A hostess from the church sits at each table. Her role is to make each person at the table feel welcome, comfortable, and valued.

The church works hard to make every aspect of the evening special, partly because most of these single moms don't have many opportunities to be pampered. More important, the underlying message is that they are loved extravagantly by a loving God.

For example, the food is wonderful. At a recent dinner in November, the menu included turkey with a special gravy, spinach and mandarin orange salad, stuffing with cranberries, garlic mashed potatoes, sweet potato cheesecake, and apple cider, tea, and coffee.

At 7:30 Nancy Wilson, who leads the outreach, announces upcoming events and options for the second hour of the evening. For example, moms might choose to take part in an active-parenting class (see page 13), accompany someone from the church to the sanctuary for individual prayer, or participate in a small-group discussion about a specific topic.

Small Group Discussions

At Vineyard, these discussions have been led by people both outside the church and inside the church. For example, a representative of a local community college discussed how single moms could find financial aid for additional schooling. A special education advocate suggested ways moms could address problems their children might be having in the school system. Women from the church led discussions on topics such as anger toward oneself and others, dating God's way, and building positive experiences during the holidays.

At 8:15, the church opens the doors to the Pink Bag Boutique. This idea arose when Nancy asked the moms to make a list of material goods that would be especially helpful to them. She then asked members of the congregation to donate the items on the list. She encourages people in the church to buy something for single moms each time they shop for their own families, saying, "If you need it, so do they." And the congregation has responded generously and consistently, donating everything from food to toiletries to books. Each month, single moms are given one shopping bag and encouraged to fill it. If items remain on the shelves after everyone has filled a bag, they're invited to return and take whatever they need until the shelves are empty. And during the weeks between the dinners, the people of the church faithfully restock the shelves with donated goods.

> **❝WE ALWAYS WISH WE HAD MORE, BUT WE DO WHAT WE CAN AND TRUST GOD TO TAKE CARE OF THE REST.❞**
> **—NANCY WILSON**
> *Single Moms Pastor*
> *Vineyard Church*
> *Ann Arbor, Michigan*

As the single moms are enjoying dinner and then fellowship, their 60 to 100 children are being fed and cared for in four separate rooms: one room for infants and children through first grade, one for second- through fifth-graders, one for middle school students, and one for high school students. A team of volunteers oversees each room, ensuring that the food and after-dinner activities are age-appropriate and appealing.

> **PART OF THE COST OF THIS MINISTRY IS THAT YOU REALLY HAVE TO ACCEPT THAT YOU CAN'T FIX ANYTHING. ALL YOU CAN DO IS BE GOD'S HANDS AND FEET AS YOU DO WHAT HE GIVES YOU TO DO.**
> —NANCY WILSON

After the moms and their children leave around 8:30, all the volunteers work together to clean up, and everyone is ready to go home by 10:00. Nancy says, "After each dinner, I feel like crying, mostly because of the love I have for these women and their bravery. Their needs are so great, and the only one they can truly count on is God. So often they ask me to pray that they will have the strength just to keep going. All I can offer is my love, whatever we can give in terms of material things—which will never be enough—and my prayers."

EXTRAORDINARY EVENINGS

Twice a year, in December and February, Nancy and her teams bless single moms with an extra-special night out. In December, they have a Christmas party. After dinner, the group gathers around a Christmas tree, the church gives the moms presents, the moms themselves have great fun with a white-elephant gift exchange, carolers sing beautiful Christmas songs, moms hear the Christmas story from the book of Luke, and moms have their photos taken in front of the tree with their children. (This last idea arose from a comment one of the moms made about not having many pictures of herself with her children, as she's the only photographer in the family.)

In February, the church treats the moms to an evening of pampering. This idea stemmed from the church's ongoing quest to show these women that they are God's beloved. Nancy and her teams are always asking, "How can single moms know how precious they are to God in the midst of the hardships they face?" So, on the second Tuesday in February of each year, the church brings in manicurists, pedicurists, makeup consultants, five hairstylists, and eight massage therapists. A harpist and flutist provide relaxing music, dinner is served buffet-style, and for the next two hours women are personally pampered in a way that most of them have never known before. At the end of one of these events, one single mom exclaimed, "This is the best evening of the year!"

STAFFING

As the ministry has grown, so has the number of volunteers necessary to its success. At this writing, Nancy oversees the entire effort, which currently requires 30 or 40 helpers each month.

- She leads a team of **table hostesses:** women from the church—some of whom are single moms themselves—who sit and eat dinner with the single moms and help to ensure a positive experience for everyone at the table.

- A team of five **chefs** plans and prepares the meals. Each is a gourmet cook who is either self-taught or has had restaurant experience.

- A team of five to eight **waitpersons,** each dressed in white shirts and black trousers or skirts, sets the tables, serves, and cleans up afterward.

- **Children's teams** work with the children while moms are enjoying an evening with their peers. Each children's room is staffed by a team dedicated to that age group. These teams work with the chefs to ensure age-appropriate meals for each age group, and they plan and guide the kids in age-appropriate after-dinner activities. These times with other children their own age has become as important to the kids as their moms' time together is to them. Kids have a great time and want to attend the monthly get-togethers as much as their moms do!

- A **prayer team** is also available to meet individually and privately with moms who ask for prayer.

- Another team leads an **active-parenting** class.

Parenting Classes

At Vineyard Ann Arbor, a team of three women teach an active-parenting class during Moms' Night Out. They utilize a combination of relational and interactive teaching methods including video, lecture, discussion, and role-playing. While moms are exploring topics such as boundary setting, consequences, goal setting, rewards, communication skills, and teaching and learning styles, their children are involved in hands-on projects that dovetail with the same topic.

Active Parenting Publishers (www.activeparenting.com) offers a wide variety of resources that can help you launch a parenting class for the single moms in your church.

BUT REMEMBER, THE MINISTRY DIDN'T START WITH 30 OR 40 HELPERS; IT HAS GROWN AND DEVELOPED OVER TIME.

SHARING THE GOSPEL

By developing loving, nurturing relationships in a warm, welcoming environment, Nancy and her team hope that the love of God will be revealed to these single moms. The single moms come from Vineyard, from other churches, and from no church at all. Some are Christians; others aren't; some are rediscovering their faith. The goal is to reach out to them, wherever they are in their faith journey, with the love of Jesus.

Each evening begins with prayer, and women are given the opportunity to pray privately with a prayer partner, but no one is pressured to participate in these activities. In December, Nancy tells the Christmas story, explaining who Jesus is and why he came. This is the one clear presentation of the gospel that occurs every year. Throughout the year, the goal is to create an environment that encourages women to at least ask questions about God. And over time, as they feel accepted and loved, they begin to reveal their hearts in the one-to-one relationships that develop in this atmosphere.

Nancy has had the privilege of leading one of these single moms to Jesus, and many moms have said that after turning their backs on God, they've renewed their relationships with him as a result of the love they've experienced through this outreach.

One of the most gratifying aspects of Moms' Night Out has been its effect on the children. Nancy reports that at least one child a year has made a faith commitment to Jesus.

RIPPLE EFFECTS

Moms' Night Out is the cornerstone of Vineyard's ministry to single moms, and it has led church members to pursue many other avenues for blessing "the fatherless and the widows" of our day.

- A **car-care ministry** offers single moms free advice in purchasing a used car as well as skilled troubleshooting, minor repairs, and tuneups.

- TUG is a **mentoring ministry for boys** of single moms.

- A **home-care ministry** provides skilled workers to assist single moms with minor home repairs.

Outreach Tip

When planning activities for single moms, be sure to provide quality child care. Without it, single moms simply won't be able to attend.

- A single moms' **Bible study** meets twice a month, on Friday evenings.

- In addition to the extra-special dinner provided in December, the church offers a variety of **Christmas blessings:**
  › Nancy sends every mom a Christmas card with a personal note and a gift certificate to a regional department store. The certificates range in value from $50 to $150, depending on the number of children each mom has at home. Nancy says, "The stories of how God has used that small gift have brought tears to my eyes every year."

  › In an effort to deepen single moms' connection to the church, small groups adopt some of the moms and their families. Each group prays for the family it has adopted and, in December, blesses the children with gifts. The group also invites the family to a member's house for a Christmas party each year.

  › Nancy has worked with a local children's store to make a "Santa tree" available to the store's customers each Christmas. Customers select tags off the tree, buy the items listed on the tags, and donate them to the church. Nancy then gives the gifts to the children of families that weren't adopted by small groups.

  › Every year the moms are blessed in ways no one expected. One year, for example, a member of the church offered to pay one month's mortgage payment for a single mom. Nancy says, "I was able to connect the giver with a mom, and joy abounded!"

All of these ideas were generated by individuals in the church who recognized the special needs of single moms and decided to help.

LESSONS LEARNED

As this ministry has developed and grown, Nancy and her teams have learned some valuable lessons.

First, they've learned that **the ministry will never get off the ground without the unwavering support of the senior pastor.** If the pastor's heart doesn't beat for this ministry, if its value isn't extolled frequently from the pulpit, it won't succeed. The senior pastor doesn't have to be intimately involved in the ministry; in fact, he or she doesn't even have to attend the monthly dinners. The pastor must, however, believe passionately in the church's efforts to reach out to today's widows and orphans and must communicate that passion frequently.

Second, Nancy and her team have learned to **guide single moms toward focusing on the blessings in their lives.** These moms are often surrounded by negativity, and it's easy for them to be caught in a negative, dark mind-set.

While the moms need to be able to share their pain, Nancy and her teams make a concerted effort to help them also recognize the positive things that are happening in their lives and to see God's hand in those blessings.

Third, they've learned that **the key to the ministry is personal relationships.** That's why the church has never advertised this outreach. It has grown because single moms have invited co-workers and friends, who in turn have invited others. Nancy says, "Without relationships, this would just be an agency."

Outreach Tip

Be sure to give newcomers a list of the names and contact information of the other single moms so they can stay in touch throughout the month and not just during Moms' Night Out.

Fourth, **the goal of this ministry is not necessarily to get single moms to come to church every Sunday;** it is to help them integrate into a caring community.

Finally, **there will be times when someone has to make tough decisions.** In Vineyard's case, that person is Nancy. Over the years, some people have tried to dominate or otherwise change the loving, supportive atmosphere that Nancy and her teams work so hard to create. Nancy has realized that part of her role as leader is to preserve what God has called the ministry to do, even when that means having difficult conversations and even asking some people not to return.

C H A P T E R   O N E
IMPLEMENTATION

HOW YOUR CHURCH CAN REACH OUT TO SINGLE MOMS

If the idea of reaching out in some way to single moms resonates with you and your church, remember these principles as you develop your own outreach:

Principle 1—Begin simply and proceed slowly, allowing the outreach to grow naturally.

Principle 2—Communicate love and acceptance in everything you do.

Principle 3—Never give unsolicited advice.

Principle 4—Communicate clearly and frequently with everyone involved—the senior pastor, church staff, volunteers, and single moms.

STEPS TO TAKE

1. Develop a mission statement for the ministry that folds into the church's overall mission statement. If the church doesn't have a vision for this outreach and if the senior pastor doesn't wholeheartedly support it, it won't succeed.

> **IF GOD IS IN IT, HE WILL BLESS IT.**
> —NANCY WILSON

2. Most churches, if they're welcoming, already have single moms attending. Figure out how to love the single moms already in your congregation, and ask God how to open the door for more.

3. Recruit a team of volunteers who want to reach out to single moms, and identify a gifted leader to head the effort. This person must be willing to let this outreach be her main focus for a while, as it requires a commitment of time, effort, and spiritual and emotional energy.

4. Begin the outreach with baby steps. Ask, "What is within our current capabilities to do? A monthly dessert? A monthly dinner made at home and transferred to the church in slow cookers? A small Bible study just for single moms?" Begin with a manageable, sustainable, growable idea.

5. Survey your congregation to ascertain how your people would be willing to help.

6. Be sure that all of your planning takes children into account. If their children aren't well-fed and nurtured while in your care, single moms won't be drawn to this outreach.

7. As the outreach develops, tell stories of how God is blessing it. Tell these stories during your worship service and whenever else it is appropriate. (Do not, however, repeat personal stories that have been related in confidence.)

8. As financial support grows, find more ways to bless single moms and their children. Vineyard Ann Arbor, for example, began by taking up an offering specifically for Moms' Night Out. The church collected $200. Their first meals were served on paper plates. As more and more moms were drawn to the program, the church increased its financial support, and Nancy and her teams found more and more ways to bless the moms.

MORE SPECIFICALLY...

If you decide to pursue the idea of providing dinner one night a month to single moms, here are specific things to do to get started:

- Ask the senior pastor to launch the outreach from the pulpit in one or a series of sermons.
- Gather a group of volunteers by publishing a survey in your church bulletin. A simple, straightforward survey might read, "I'd be willing to provide:

  ❑ a main dish   ❑ once a year

  ❑ a side dish   ❑ twice a year

  ❑ a salad   ❑ several times a year."

  ❑ a dessert for Moms' Night Out

Ask for the name, phone number, and e-mail address of each respondent.

- Compile the survey results. Begin to form your team by following up with a phone call or e-mail to each person who has offered to help.

- Use your church bulletin to invite single moms to a night out. Emphasize that the evening will include dinner and age-appropriate activities for their children, in addition to dinner and fellowship for the moms themselves. Tell them that they must reserve a spot for themselves and their children by a certain date; be sure their reservations include their children's ages.

Assign your team of volunteers the following tasks:

- Take moms' reservations and ascertain the number of moms and children (by age group) who will be attending.

- Plan menus for moms and children. (Remember to keep menus uncomplicated when you're first getting started. A menu might be as simple as sloppy joes, a salad, bags of chips, brownies, lemonade, coffee, and tea. See Chapter 3, "Reach Out to High School Students," for simple menu ideas.)

- Call survey respondents to assign food-preparation tasks. Be sure to specify the amount of food each volunteer must prepare and where and when it is to be dropped off. (If your church doesn't have a refrigerator, the food will have to be dropped off within 30 minutes of the beginning of the meal.)

- Set up tables and chairs, set the tables, serve the meal, clean up afterward.

- Act as table hostesses.

- Oversee children's meals and plan age-appropriate activities for kids after dinner. (At first, the number of children will probably be relatively small, so all of the children will be grouped together. The challenge is to find activities that children of varying ages will enjoy. Find ways to engage the older children in helping the younger ones.)

You and your team of volunteers will probably begin by providing a lot of items from your own homes. Over time, as the outreach grows, more and more material things—such as dinnerware, table linens, and cooking facilities—will probably be provided by the church. While it's important to honor single moms and their children with the best your church can provide, the heart and soul of this outreach is the welcoming spirit these moms and their kids will feel the moment they step into your church.

FINAL THOUGHTS ABOUT...VOLUNTEERS

The job of reaching out to single moms is too big for one person to undertake alone. Nancy Wilson offers the following tips for recruiting and maintaining a committed team of volunteers:

1. Give potential volunteers a chance to see the outreach at work before asking them to commit to it. Most single moms are going through difficult times, and spending time with them is not all hearts and roses. Volunteers who have a realistic idea of the ministry before they sign on are more likely to stick with it.

2. Check in frequently with teams of volunteers. This will allow you to uncover problems before they become overwhelming. Volunteers tend to suffer in silence and finally give up; staying in close touch with them will help you put out small fires before they get out of control.

3. Finally, the best way to encourage your team is to tell the stories you hear from single moms each week. This, more than any thing, keeps volunteers coming back.

"RELIGION THAT GOD OUR FATHER ACCEPTS AS PURE AND FAULTLESS IS THIS: TO LOOK AFTER ORPHANS AND WIDOWS IN THEIR DISTRESS AND TO KEEP ONESELF FROM BEING POLLUTED BY THE WORLD."
—JAMES 1:27

REACH OUT
THROUGH SPORTS

In only four years, this church has seen nearly 1,000 people make a faith commitment through its sports outreach.

☑ BUILDS AUTHENTIC RELATIONSHIPS
☑ CAN REACH AN ENTIRE COMMUNITY
☑ APPEALS TO UNCHURCHED CHILDREN AND ADULTS
☑ BUILDS A STRONG SENSE OF COMMUNITY

THE EVOLUTION OF THE IDEA

W hen staff members at First Baptist Church in Oviedo, Florida, think about outreach, they think big. They wonder, "How can we touch an entire community with the message of Jesus?" One of their most successful methods of reaching the nearly 30,000 residents of Oviedo is through sports.

Here is their rationale: Oviedo is a growing community, and much of the growth is coming from young families that are moving into the area. If families are churchgoers, they'll visit churches in the area until they find the right one for them. But what about families who aren't churchgoers, aren't Christian, or profess no faith at all? These families—like the churchgoing families—will often investigate the recreational opportunities available to their children. A church that provides high-quality sports programs will gain an immediate entry point into the lives of the newcomers. What's more, families are likely to remain connected to a church whose sports are distinguished by an emphasis on sportsmanlike behavior and Christ-like values.

Makes sense. And it has proved to be true. In 2001, the church had 300 to 400 people involved in all of its sports programs. By the end of 2005, it had over 5,000. And in those four years, the church saw nearly 1,000 people touched by those programs make a faith commitment to Jesus Christ.

THE GOAL

According to David Erdmann, minister of sports and recreation at First Baptist, the church's sports ministry unfolds in three stages: First, through its sports offerings, the church is made more visible to the community; second, through their children's involvement in these sports, the parents of both church families and newcomers get to know one another; and third, as relationships develop between both sets of families, the church begins to minister to the families who aren't otherwise connected to the church. In short, sports have proven to be the easiest way for the community to get to know the people of First Baptist.

And a church doesn't have to have a gym, expansive grounds, and a huge budget to use sports as an outreach tool. For example, a church plant on Staten Island began its sports ministry with three-on-three basketball tournaments in the projects—a very inexpensive way to gain exposure to the community while serving kids. The outreach began when the church had three members. Three and a half years later, it had a membership of 180.

WHERE TO START?

The key, according to David Erdmann, is to identify an unmet need and find a way to meet it. For example, in his church's case, the community already had many thriving sports leagues for children and adults. So he asked, "What can we do that's not being done?" When he discovered that there were no opportunities for preschoolers to get involved in sports in Oviedo, he started to think about the games that preschoolers can play, and soccer came to mind.

In Florida, soccer is hugely popular with children, but the game is played outdoors under the hot sun, and young children, who haven't yet acquired the fine-motor skills to play well, spend a lot of time running up and down long fields, kicking the ball out of bounds. It's tiring for the kids and boring for their parents on the sidelines. So First Baptist decided to offer an indoor soccer league in an air-conditioned space for children from 3½ years through third grade. It was an immediate hit. In this setting, the children learn the game faster, and the parents can cheer them on in comfort.

Then David started considering how to involve young children in baseball. The community had a strong Little League and Babe Ruth League, but nothing for preschoolers. So he started a T-ball league, again for children from 3½ years through third grade. It's now the largest T-ball league in Seminole County.

NOT JUST SPORTS

But offering the children of a community a place to play sports can be done by any number of secular organizations. What distinguishes First Baptist's sports leagues from those offered by the community? One thing: its firm insistence on Christ-like behavior on and off the playing field, on the court as well as in the bleachers.

Recognizing that "when people walk into a gym, they lose their minds," David has launched an all-out effort to retrain adults in appropriate sports-related conduct and to instill these values in their children. It's a part of everything his ministry does. For example, he requires every athlete and every parent to sign a code of conduct. He teaches a course for parents called How to Raise a Christian Athlete. He teaches them that their role is to be cheerleaders, not coaches. If they want to coach, there are plenty of opportunities for them to become trained for this role. But if they are there strictly as parents, their job is to be cheerleaders. And good cheerleaders are always happy. They cheer for both teams equally. They engender an atmosphere of encouragement.

Whether or not parents attend David's class, they're required to come to a meeting at the beginning of each season, in which these values are restated. The constant, unchanging message is "For sports to be win-win, everyone has to be involved in a positive way."

A MULTITUDE OF OPPORTUNITIES

There are lots of ways to reach the community through sports. Here are just a few.

Basketball—This is one of the easiest sports for a church to sponsor because it's popular among all age groups, requires little in the way of equipment, and can be adapted to many settings. A multipurpose room, even with industrial-grade carpet, can act as a court, using taped-off boundaries and portable hoops. As few as eight people can form a team, and a league can be started with as few as 60.

First Baptist currently sponsors a wide variety of leagues: one for 4-year-olds, one for kindergartners, and one for each grade through fifth. The church used to sponsor a middle school league but discovered that by the time children reach middle school, they want to move into the city leagues, which they consider more competitive, and they're not nearly as interested in having their parents watch them play. Because families weren't involved, the outreach wasn't as strong. So now the church offers an open gym to middle schoolers on Friday nights, giving them the opportunity to hang out with their friends and play basketball, volleyball, and Xbox games.

The church also sponsors high school and adult leagues during the off-season (March, April, and May). This league reaches men rather than families, and is extremely successful. In fact, the adult league is one of the most competitive in the area and includes semipro and college players. Even so, the message is still "Everything done in this gym must be God-honoring," and it is well known that the church has zero tolerance for unsportsmanlike behavior. If, for example, an adult commits a technical foul, he must leave the gym immediately. If he commits a second technical foul during the season, he is expelled from the league and won't be readmitted for two years.

The church has found three-on-three tournaments to be great one-time events for adults, high school students, and middle school students. People form their own teams for this event, which is usually held on a Saturday during spring break or in the summer. Because it's an exciting one-day event, families come to watch, and the opportunities for mingling with families outside the church are increased.

Three-on-three tournaments are popular for several reasons. They appeal to groups of best friends who think they can take on the world. The games are fast-paced, lasting only 15 minutes, and full of exciting offensive moves (everyone is shooting all the time). They are played on half-courts, so the venue can accommodate twice as many teams. They're also easy to organize and inexpensive. A church can charge each entrant $10, which covers the cost of the referees, T-shirts for all participants, and trophies.

Cheerleading—According to the "2004 Sports Participation in America Report" sponsored by the Sporting Goods Manufacturers Association, cheerleading in the United States grows by nearly 50 percent each year, and 1.4 million cheerleaders are between 6 and 11 years old.

It's no wonder then that, after basketball, cheerleading is the most popular sport at First Baptist. The church sponsors cheerleading leagues during high school basketball season (November through February). These leagues offer girls from 3½ years of age through fifth grade another way to get involved in sports, and they love it.

Because cheerleading is notoriously expensive, the church orders its uniforms, poms, megaphones, and other equipment through an evangelistic sports ministry called Upward (www.upward.org), which is able to buy these items in huge quantities and sell them to churches for much less than the churches could purchase them on their own.

In Florida, Pop Warner cheerleading camps are enormously popular, and waiting lists are long. David's church worked with Upward to develop an alternative that includes sportsmanlike cheers and conservative uniforms and always promotes Upward's belief that "every child is a winner." The families of First Baptist are especially grateful for this healthy alternative for their children.

Soccer—Soccer is a very popular sport among children, especially in the Sun Belt. If a church doesn't have its own field, it's often easy to gain access to public fields. For example, a church could approach a school and ask to use the school's soccer fields during weekends.

At First Baptist of Oviedo, the church uses its own indoor facilities and has leagues for children from 3½ years of age through fifth grade. The leagues are formed by age level, so the pre-kindergartners play together, the first-graders play together, and so on. The church might combine fourth- and fifth-graders in one league, depending on the number of kids in the program.

Baseball—This is a relatively easy sport for a church to sponsor, as long as the church has access to a field. Because liability insurance is more expensive for baseball, smaller churches are sometimes unable to offer it.

Coaching

Coaching is the most important role in a sports ministry. Almost anyone who has been involved in American sports can tell horror stories about the negative influence of harsh, demanding, win-at-any-cost coaches on their lives or those of their children. Coaches, for better or worse, have a tremendous impact on children's lives. But imagine if children were coached only by caring, capable people, who held Christ pre-eminent in their lives. Imagine if they were taught from the time they could dribble or throw a ball how to glorify God on the court or playing field. What better way to influence kids' lives than through exemplary Christian coaches?

And a good coach doesn't have to have a deep understanding of the game. According to David Erdmann, coaches must, above all, know how to teach; they can always be shown what to teach.

In any church-sponsored sports program, it is essential to provide a safe environment for children and to promote it. That's why First Baptist conducts extensive background checks, including a full criminal check, drug screening, and reference check, of all coaches. (Log on to www.churchvolunteercentral.com for a good source of background checks tailored especially to the church.)

Flag Football—Flag football is an inexpensive, safe alternative to regular football, and more and more churches are offering flag football leagues for children as young as first grade. Some churches also offer adult leagues with great success. In those leagues, the majority of the families are church families, so if a church wants to provide a recreation ministry for its members, adult flag football is a great choice. But if a sports ministry is intended to reach the community outside of the church, David Erdmann has found that flag football may not be as effective with adults as it is with children.

5K Race/Walk—Offering people the chance to take part in a running event is a great way to get the church's name in front of the community. While it doesn't foster long-term relationships in the way that team sports do, it does increase the community's awareness of the church and creates goodwill. It's especially attractive to smaller churches that don't have the facilities to offer ongoing sports leagues.

SHARING THE GOSPEL

By concentrating on youth sports, David Erdmann and his coaches, referees, and team moms have gotten to know children and their families in ways that wouldn't be possible in other settings. Twice a week for 10 weeks, they have access to these kids, talking with them, getting to know them, loving and encouraging them. In fact, these leagues aren't about sports nearly as much as they are about relationships.

> **"PEOPLE KNOW US AND KNOW WE LOVE THEM. WHEN THEY NEED US, THEY KNOW WE'RE HERE."**
> —DAVID ERDMANN
> *Minister of Sports and Recreation*
> *First Baptist Church*
> *Oviedo, Florida*

Here's an example. A family from First Baptist invited its neighbors to enter their 3½-year-old boy in the church's T-ball league. The neighbors were nominal Christians, but they weren't churchgoers, and Christianity didn't seem to play a role in their lives. They signed their son up for T-ball, and the mom attended his games, but the dad didn't. At the end of the season, David Erdmann got a call from a friend telling him that the little boy had suffered a terrible eye injury at home. David went to the hospital and found that the boy was in the intensive care unit, and the doctors worried that he might lose his eye. During the long hours of waiting and recovery, the church rallied around this family, providing home-cooked meals, caring for the family's other children—showing God's love in all the practical ways they could think of. And it had a profound effect on the parents, who have since become church members and are now professing Christians. They've told all of their friends about the love and support the people of First Baptist showered upon them in their time of need. David says, "This is why we do what we do. It's all about relationships."

RIPPLE EFFECTS

Through its sports ministry in its own community, First Baptist of Oviedo has discovered the power of sports in the international missions field. According to David Erdmann, "People involved in sports speak a universal language. I have walked onto a basketball court in Russia, played four hours of basketball without speaking a word of Russian, and at the end of the day sat down and shared the gospel through an interpreter. Because I had earned the players' respect on the court, they were willing to listen to me. Sports is the easiest way I know to break down language, religious, ethnic, and racial barriers."

LESSONS LEARNED

The sports ministry at First Baptist of Oviedo has been phenomenally successful for several reasons.

First, **the church hired someone to spearhead the effort who knows sports and is passionate about sports ministry.** David Erdmann's goal is to find every possible way to reach the community through sports. So the church's sports facilities are busy most hours of the night and day, and David and his staff are always looking for fresh ways to reach the community.

Second, they've learned that **proper planning and timing are key to success.** They've learned not to jump into something without satisfactorily answering these questions: Will this event serve a need in the community? Can we do it well? Do we have the expertise or access to the expertise to do this? What will it cost? Do we have the leadership to pull it off? They've learned that *wanting* to do something isn't sufficient reason to do it; they must also conclude that they *should* and *can* do it.

Third, **they've learned the importance of convincing the entire church family of the value of the ministry.** Because this ministry requires so much lay leadership in the form of coaches, assistant coaches, team moms, referees, and support personnel, it's not a matter of selling the idea to a few people on a committee. It requires churchwide support.

Volunteers

Leadership is crucial to a successful sports ministry, and a common mistake is to underestimate the number of leaders a church will need to pull it off.

David Erdmann offers this example. In 2005, he had a pre-K co-ed basketball division consisting of 10 teams. Each team required a coach, an assistant coach (while a coach is on the floor, an assistant coach must oversee the kids on the bench), and a team mom. (The team mom is responsible for communicating with the other moms and arranging the snack rotation. She's the one who ensures that

(Continued on next page.)

Volunteers

(Continued from previous page.)

people are where they're supposed to be when they're supposed to be there.) So this one division alone required an initial commitment by 30 volunteers. Since each team consisted of about 10 children, David had a ready supply of parents whose shoulders he could tap for these three roles.

In addition, he needed people to supervise practices during the week, two or three people to set up the gym on Saturday morning, referees, two or three people to announce the games, and two or three others to greet people and man the concession stand. Some of these people can do double duty; still, for this one division alone, David needed to recruit 30 to 40 volunteers.

But at the same time, they've learned to trust God for the outcome. David says, "The first year, you can't find enough coaches, but somehow, God provides them. After proper planning, you have to trust that this is a God-given vision and relax."

CHAPTER TWO
IMPLEMENTATION

HOW YOUR CHURCH CAN REACH OUT THROUGH SPORTS

If this idea resonates with you and your church, remember these principles as you develop your own sports ministry:

Principle 1—Ensure that Christ-like behavior is the hallmark of your program, on and off the playing field.

Principle 2—Offer high-quality programs. If the quality of coaching, refereeing, uniforms, and equipment is not as high as that of secular alternatives, people outside of the church won't be attracted to the program.

Principle 3—Be sure that at least half of the participants—on the court and in the bleachers—are church families so that they can be salt and light to those who aren't.

> **IF GOD'S INVOLVED, IT'LL WORK.**
> —DAVID ERDMANN

STEPS TO TAKE

1. Pray. Ask God to guide you every step of the way.

2. Establish your vision for a sports ministry. You might consider two avenues: a positive recreation ministry for church families or an outreach to the community. If your vision is to reach out to the community, take the following steps.

3. Meet with someone who has experience with a sports outreach, and pick this person's brain. Contact Upward (www.upward.org) to find the name of someone in your area who has this kind of experience and can help you get started.

4. Find out what's going on in your community. Which sports and age groups are being served well? Which aren't?

5. Evaluate your church's facilities. Do you have an underused multipurpose building? an empty lot that could be turned into an athletic field? access to sports venues through your community's schools or parks?

6. Assess your people. How willing and able are they to undertake this outreach? Do you have the lay leadership necessary to provide coaching? Are your members willing to volunteer as referees, team moms, announcers, greeters, concession workers, and practice supervisors? Are parents willing to befriend the parents of non-church children, inviting them into their lives?

7. Consider your budget. What will the initial outreach cost? What are secular sports leagues charging for a similar event? Will your church be able to charge enough to pay for the event, or will it have to supplement the event with its own funds? If the latter, where will those funds come from?

8. Convey your vision for a sports ministry to the entire church. Without the church's support, the effort won't get off the ground.

9. If your church has fewer than 1,000 members, consider purchasing an all-inclusive program to help you get started. Because they're able to buy in bulk, these "sports in a box" programs offer you the quality of a large program at the cost of a small one. Upward, for example, provides everything from leadership training to equipment kits—including youth basketball, cheerleading, soccer, and flag football director manuals and DVDs, coach and referee training, advertising brochures and posters, uniforms, Bibles, devotions, and a multitude of other items. Because Upward buys 200,000 of these items at a time, it's able to provide them to individual churches at lower costs than the churches could negotiate on their own.

10. Start small, doing whatever will be most effective in your community that you can do with excellence.

11. Build your program through word-of-mouth advertising. You'll know the program is succeeding if it's growing only through the referrals of people who have been involved in it.

FINAL THOUGHTS ABOUT...EARNING THE RIGHT TO SHARE YOUR FAITH

David Erdmann says, "Sometimes we're intimidated by the idea of sharing our faith and standing out because we're Christians. The challenge is, we're called to do it anyway. So how can we do that? I've found that one of the most effective ways is through sports ministry. It's a nonconfrontational way to show Christ's love. If we show people we love them, they'll want to know why. They'll ask, 'Why are you willing to go to all of this trouble to serve me and my family?' At that point, we've earned the right to tell them. I know very few people who are unwilling to share their faith when asked."

REACH OUT TO HIGH SCHOOL STUDENTS

A couple of compassionate moms bring a high school and a church together to serve students a free lunch each week.

- ☑ APPEALS TO UNCHURCHED YOUTH
- ☑ EASY TO IMPLEMENT
- ☑ BRIDGES THE GAP BETWEEN CHURCHES AND SCHOOLS
- ☑ BUILDS AUTHENTIC RELATIONSHIPS
- ☑ CAN BE DONE BY A FEW VOLUNTEERS

THE EVOLUTION OF THE IDEA

Greeley Central is the oldest high school in Greeley, Colorado, and it is situated less than a block from Christ Community Church, one of the oldest churches in this city of 100,000. Both have existed next to each other for over 50 years, but, until 2004, there had never been an intentional outreach from the church to the students, at least one that current church leadership could remember.

Senior high youth pastor K.J. Tencza was looking for a way to reach out to these 1,300 students, who form the most diverse student body in the city, and include urban and rural teenagers, the children of migrants and the children of doctors. As K.J. was praying for a way to reach out to them, two parents were yearning to do the same thing.

Willma Heckman was looking for a way to reach the students at Greeley Central, her son's school; her friend Rhonda Zehrbach was looking for a service project for her two adolescent children, whom she home schools. Rhonda attends Christ Community Church, and Willma attends a church across town. They put their heads together and then contacted K.J. at the church and Mary Lauer, the high school's principal.

Their idea was simple: Provide a free lunch to any student in the school once a week in the church's youth room. The principal loved the idea of a safe place within walking distance of the school, where students could get away from the school environment, relax, and enjoy a break from cafeteria food once a week. K.J. was delighted with the opportunity to show these students, many of whom have never stepped inside a church, that the church can be a safe, fun, cool place to hang out. By seeing to students' physical needs for food and safe shelter, Willma and Rhonda hoped to pique their curiosity enough to prompt them to ask, "Why do you do this? What motivates you?"

Dubbing the program "Lunch Baux," they served their first lunch in October 2004. They prepared sloppy joes and all the fixings for 50. One solitary student showed up. Undaunted, Willma and Rhonda talked to teachers and band members about the free lunch and asked them to spread the word. (Willma is a "band mom," who knows the members of the high school band and relates well with them.) The next week, eight students came.

ESTABLISHING TRUST

In spite of a slow start, the word got around within a few weeks that every Thursday the church was offering a cool alternative to the cafeteria. By January, Willma, Rhonda, and four other volunteers were serving lunch to 120 students every week. Now, visit the youth room at Christ Community Church during lunchtime on Thursdays during the school year, and you'll find the room filled to capacity with youth of all stripes: boys sporting lettermen's jackets, Goths, students wearing skater pants and chains, cheerleaders, punks, and anarchists. About half of the youth are Christians or nominal Christians. The rest are unchurched. All are welcome, and all know it.

The room is dimly lit and features comfortable couches as well as bistro seating, loud music, and plasma TVs showing music videos. Students start arriving at 11:15, and by 11:20 a line snakes out the door and up the steps from this basement room. By 11:30 the room is full of energy and laughter. This is not a fluorescent dome of awkwardness; this is *not* your average high school cafeteria.

ASKED WHY HE COMES EACH WEEK, ONE BOY SPREAD HIS ARMS AND SAID, "WHERE ELSE COULD I FIND ALL OF THIS?"

When most students have gotten their food and are seated, K.J. asks a different student each week to pray. Youths wearing hats voluntarily remove them, all bow their heads, everyone listens to the prayer, and lunch resumes.

Regardless of their backgrounds, students are respectful of the property, picking up dropped food, taking dirty dishes to the trash, and thanking those who served them. Early in the program, some students asked if they could make donations to help defray costs; now a basket at one end of the cafeteria-style line collects about $30 a week.

By 11:50, the room has cleared, and volunteers are tying up trash bags and washing platters and serving utensils in the kitchen. By 12:15, the room is swept and straightened, the kitchen is clean, and the volunteers are finished for the week. It's an hour-and-a-half sprint that leaves the volunteers tired but at the same time energized and satisfied.

SHARING THE GOSPEL

One of the reasons students were initially hesitant to cross the street for a free lunch was that they thought they would be greeted with a sermon. When told about the program, their first question was, "Will they preach at me?"

During the first year, K.J. recruited three youth leaders from his church to be available during these lunches. In appearance, they can easily be mistaken for high school or college students. Their job is simply to hang out and get to know the youth. Students who are curious bring up spiritual matters, but the youth leaders don't lead the discussion.

The volunteers serving lunch have become well-known to the students, who call them by name, joke around with them, and sometimes hug them before leaving. It's clear that the students have come to know and trust the adults involved in the outreach.

As a result, some, who had never attended church, now consider Christ Community their home church. One girl sought out K.J. and asked why the church was offering free lunches. As they talked, she began to tell him about her troubled life, including a recent abortion. She has since become a member of K.J.'s youth group.

While it's still important that the teenagers don't feel ambushed by a hidden agenda, K.J. feels that, to be effective, at some point the outreach should address spiritual matters. Now that the program is in its second year and students have learned to trust the people at the church, K.J. has begun to pose a thought-provoking question each Thursday, such as "Do all religions lead to heaven?" or "From where does religion come?" Small cards with the question written on them are placed on each table. There is no formal discussion, just a written question at each table. Students often ignore the questions, but sometimes the questions lead to discussions and even to heated debate. K.J.'s goal is to get youth thinking about spiritual issues and to show them that the church is a safe place in which to debate them.

RIPPLE EFFECTS

One of the most interesting offshoots of this outreach has been the teachers' positive response. They've heard so much enthusiastic feedback from students that they've asked to join them! To maintain the "escape from school" aspect of the event, K.J. and his volunteers are planning a separate experience for teachers and staff. They'll serve them the same menu but in a different, quieter room.

Students from another high school in Greeley have heard about the program and have begun to attend as well. For many of the students from both high schools, their willingness to venture onto church property represents a huge step in itself. Some are beginning to realize that church might be a viable option for them.

In fact, one of K.J.'s senior high youth groups has seen significant growth. Until recently, the average attendance at Sunday night get-togethers averaged 60, but recently that number has increased to 70 or 80. Many of the new students were introduced to the church through Lunch Baux.

The program has also created a new team of people representing churches throughout the city. Volunteers from nearly a dozen churches have formed friendships with other parent volunteers. Some of these parents home school their children and have used Lunch Baux as a service opportunity for them. This, in turn, has allowed the home-schooled children to interact with students from the public school system, mitigating stereotypes and forging new friendships among the high schoolers as well.

Finally, the outreach has created a spirit of cooperation between the school and the church as both work together for the students. At the end of the school year, the principal sent the church an enormous—and very expensive—bouquet along with a letter thanking the church for this outreach and asking, "How can I help? My office is right across the street, and I'm here from 8:00 until 5:00." In turn, K.J. is considering providing hot meals and cots to the football team on Friday nights before games. The school and the church are learning that there are many opportunities for cooperation.

LESSONS LEARNED

When asked what he would do differently if he were to begin this outreach now, K.J. replies, "I would have formed a better alliance with the high school by volunteering there, maybe as a cafeteria monitor or hall monitor. We in the church expect people to come to us instead of going to them. I've learned to meet people where they are before I can expect them to come to church. It's so ingrained in us to believe that people have to come to church to see Jesus, when in fact, he's in the high school, too. As Christians, we have to show people where he is."

IMPLEMENTATION

HOW YOUR CHURCH CAN REACH OUT TO HIGH SCHOOL STUDENTS

If this idea resonates with you and your church, remember these principles as you develop your own outreach:

Principle 1—Form an alliance with the high school before embarking on the outreach; then work with the principal to promote it.

Principle 2— Create a physical atmosphere to which youth will be drawn.

Principle 3—Provide generous portions of homemade food.

Principle 4—Prompt students to begin to think about spiritual matters, but don't force or lead the discussion.

"MEET PEOPLE WHERE THEY ARE."
—K.J. TENCZA
Senior High Youth Pastor
Christ Community Church
Greeley, Colorado

REMEMBER THESE THINGS

For this outreach to be successful, **the food must be tasty and plentiful.** Something as simple as nachos can be made special by loading up the nachos with seasoned ground beef, refried beans, cheese, salsa, jalapeños, and sour cream. And it's important that the desserts be homemade. Brownies and cookies are always a hit. Even chocolate pudding can be jazzed up by topping it with crushed Oreo cookies and whipped cream. The point is to use the quality of the food to show students that you care for them.

To ensure that there's enough food to go around and no one goes back to school hungry, **prepare half again the number of servings you think you'll need.** Have volunteers serve the food, giving one serving the first time through. After everyone has been served, allow anyone who wants more to have a second helping.

Provide meat-free alternatives for vegetarian students. This is usually a simple matter of eliminating the meat in a small portion of the entrees. With each of the main courses listed on pages 40-43, we've also suggested a meat-free alternative.

In planning your menus, remember to **keep it simple.** Students are happy with only lemonade and water to choose between for a beverage.

STAFFING

This outreach may be accomplished by a few committed volunteers. At Christ Community Church, two parents spearhead the effort. They plan the menus, shop for groceries, prepare most of the food, recruit other parents to prepare and deliver the desserts, and recruit four volunteers to help them serve and clean up each week. Shopping takes about two hours a week; cooking takes four to six, depending on the menu; and assembling and serving the food and cleaning up take a group of six about two hours. (Much of the food preparation is done at home; the food is then reheated and assembled at the church.)

But to lessen the burden, it would be easy to recruit more volunteers. For example, one person might be responsible for planning and recruiting; one for shopping; two or three for cooking; two for making desserts; and six for assembling, serving, and cleaning up. This way, no one would have to devote more than two hours every week to the outreach.

> **"I JUST SHOW UP. THE VOLUNTEERS DO ALL THE WORK."**
> —K.J. TENCZA

MENU IDEAS

The volunteers at Christ Community have developed 10 entrees that the teenagers love and are affordable and easy to prepare. The entrees are always accompanied by a salad and a homemade dessert.

Salad—Washed, bagged salad greens are bought in bulk, and bacon bits, cheese, and croutons are always provided, as they're popular and easy to store. Other vegetables, such as tomatoes and onions—items with short shelf lives—are usually not provided unless they're being served in conjunction with the entree. Ranch dressing is by far the most popular salad dressing, and it is available in gallon jugs. Consider providing other varieties, such as Italian, Thousand Island, and French, in smaller containers.

Entrees—The following are suggestions for 10 main dishes, tips for their preparation, and vegetarian alternatives. Experiment with these ideas, adapting them to your setting, the number of people you're serving, and their preferences. And be creative! Your church is probably full of wonderful cooks who have terrific ideas for food that teenagers will love.

1. Loaded Nachos

This is one of the most popular Lunch Baux entrees. As students enter the serving line, they find salad, then the following nacho ingredients. They tell the servers what they want, and the servers ladle out the requested ingredients, which helps control portions. (Dessert and beverages are always located at the end of the serving line.)

- Tortilla chips
- Browned ground beef seasoned with taco seasoning
- Vegetarian refried beans (served from slow cookers or electric roasters to keep them warm)
- Nacho cheese sauce (served from slow cookers to keep it warm)
- Salsa
- Jalapeños
- Sour cream

Shopping Tip

- Whenever possible, purchase food and staples, such as taco seasoning, in bulk.

Preparation Tips

- Remove fat from ground beef and eliminate a greasy mess on your stove by browning the meat in a microwave. Place 1 pound of ground beef at a time in a microwave-safe colander; then place the colander inside a microwave-safe bowl. Cook on high for 2 minutes. Crumble with a fork. Cook on high for 2 more minutes. Stir. Cook 2 minutes more. This method allows most of the fat to drain into the bowl. Refrigerate or freeze the ground beef until you're ready to use it. The morning of the lunch, place the thawed meat in large pans, season with taco seasoning, and reheat. (One pound of ground beef will serve 7 to 8 students.)
- In the morning, place nacho cheese sauce in a slow cooker to heat it thoroughly. Extend the sauce by adding 1 to 1½ cups of milk to each #10 can of cheese sauce.
- Heat and serve refried beans from a slow cooker or an electric roaster. (Refer to the directions on the label to determine how many cans of beans you'll need for your group.)

Vegetarian alternative—nachos without the beef

2. Burritos

This recipe allows you to use refried beans and ground beef left over from the day you served nachos. In fact, it's a great idea to cook twice as much ground beef as you'll need for the nachos in order to save this step when preparing burritos. The browned meat freezes well.

Preparation Tips

- Combine browned ground beef with refried beans, using a ratio of 5 pounds of beef for every #10 can of refried beans. (You can reduce costs and make the meat go further by changing the ratio to 3 pounds of beef to every #10 can of beans.)
- Roll the ground beef and bean mixture into soft tortillas; then roll each in a small aluminum foil sheet and freeze.
- The day before the event, thaw the burritos.
- The day of the event, place the foil-wrapped burritos on cookie sheets and heat at 350 degrees for 30 to 50 minutes, or until warm.
- Serve with salsa, shredded cheese, jalapeños, sour cream, and green chili sauce (available precooked in jars from most grocery stores).

Vegetarian alternative—bean and cheese burritos

3. Pasta

This is an easy dish to prepare and tastes homemade with the addition of extra seasonings. Serve the pasta with hamburger buns that you've sliced in half, sprinkled with garlic powder and basil, and then broiled until lightly browned.

Preparation Tips

(For every 45 students, you'll need 2 pounds of ground beef, a #10 can of spaghetti sauce, and an 8-pound bag of penne pasta.)

- Brown ground beef. Add spaghetti sauce. Season with garlic salt and Italian seasoning to taste. Refrigerate until the morning of the event.
- Reheat the sauce in large pots.
- Cook penne pasta in boiling water, following package directions.
- In a large electric roaster, combine 1 pot of meat sauce with 1 package of cooked pasta. Serve from the electric roaster. Combine the remainder of the sauce and pasta as needed. (If you combine them all at once, the pasta will absorb moisture from the sauce and become sticky.)

Vegetarian alternative—meatless spaghetti sauce

4. Hot Dogs

Grilled hot dogs are so much more appealing and tasty than their boiled counterparts. So plan to grill the hot dogs a day or two before the event; then warm them thoroughly in an electric roaster before serving. The key to making this meal special is to grill the meat and to have lots of condiments—including pickle relish, mustard, ketchup, mayonnaise, sauerkraut, and onions—a wide variety of chips, and, of course, great homemade desserts.

Vegetarian alternative—tofu hot dogs

5. Hamburgers

Like hot dogs, hamburgers are much tastier when they're grilled rather than fried, and they can be grilled beforehand and reheated the day of the event. Be sure to offer chips, pickle spears, and lots of condiments, including lettuce and sliced tomatoes.

Vegetarian alternative—veggie hamburgers

6. Breakfast Casseroles

The volunteers at Christ Community developed this main dish after several students requested breakfast entrees. Instead of a green salad, the volunteers serve fresh fruit (such as apples, oranges, and bananas), and instead of lemonade, they serve a breakfast drink such as Tang. They also offer bagels, cream cheese, and butter.

Shopping Tip

Be on the lookout for eggs on sale before preparing this entree.

Preparation Tips

(Each pan will yield 18 servings.)

- The day before the event, combine 2 pounds thawed, grated hash browns with 1 stick melted butter or margarine. Press the mixture into the bottom of a large disposable aluminum steamer pan. (First be sure the pan will fit into your oven!) Bake at 400 degrees for 30 minutes or until edges are slightly browned.
- Fry 1 pound bacon, sausage, or diced ham. Crumble bacon or sausage; sprinkle meat on top of hash brown mixture. Add chopped green chilies, diced onions, and 2 cups shredded cheddar cheese. Refrigerate. (If you're making several casseroles, spread wax paper over the hash brown mixture and stack the pans inside of each other to maximize room in your refrigerator.)
- Beat 12 eggs with 2 cups milk and salt and pepper to taste. Refrigerate. (Plastic milk jugs make great storage containers for this mixture.)
- The day of the event, pour the egg mixture over the hash brown mixture. Bake at 375 to 400 degrees for 45 to 60 minutes, until lightly browned and a knife inserted into the center comes out clean.

Vegetarian alternative—In one casserole, substitute a 15-ounce can drained, diced tomatoes for the meat.

7. Sloppy Joes

Use your favorite sloppy joe recipe, using ground beef. Serve on buns along with pickle spears and assorted chips.

Vegetarian alternative—veggie hamburgers or tofu hot dogs

8. Soup and Sandwiches

This can be more expensive than the other main dishes because of the high price of lunchmeat.

Sandwiches—Set out kaiser rolls, mayonnaise, and mustard. Provide an assortment of lunchmeats, such as ham, turkey, and salami, along with sliced cheese, lettuce leaves, and sliced tomatoes and onions. Offer pickle spears and an assortment of chips as well.

Soup—Vegetable beef and chicken noodle are popular choices among teenagers. The volunteers at Christ Community use their favorite recipes, multiplying ingredients according to the number of students they plan to serve.

Vegetarian alternative—cheese sandwiches and tomato soup

9. Salad and Baked Potato Bar

Provide one large baked potato per student and a wide variety of condiments, such as steamed broccoli with cheese, chili, shredded cheese, butter, sour cream, and salsa. (Don't forget salt and pepper!) Ask students to suggest other toppings, and modify your offerings throughout the year.

Expand the salad bar to include items such as tomatoes, cucumbers, beets, garbanzo beans, and olives.

Preparation Tips

Wrap potatoes in foil and roast for 2½ hours before the event. Or you may roast the potatoes several days in advance and reheat them in an oven or electric roaster. To keep potatoes warm, serve them from an electric roaster.

10. Chili Fritos

According to a recent Lunch Baux questionnaire, this is the most popular main dish among the students who responded to the survey. It consists of chili served over a bed of Fritos corn chips, topped with shredded cheddar cheese. Jalapeños and chopped onions are available for those who want them. You may make your own chili or buy it in industrial-size cans and heat it. (Each can will serve 13 to 15 students. Leftover chili can be used on the days you serve hot dogs or baked potatoes.)

Vegetarian alternative—vegetarian chili, available in 15-ounce cans

BUDGETING

At the beginning of the program, the church asked for a $3 donation from each student to cover the cost of the groceries. As the program grew and the church recognized the value of this outreach, the cost of the groceries was added to the church's annual budget, and the students now eat for free. Each week the volunteers buy the groceries, submit their receipts, and are reimbursed by the church.

FINAL THOUGHTS ABOUT...REACHING TODAY'S YOUTH

If you were to listen to some of the conversations around Lunch Baux tables, K.J. Tencza says you would hear discussions about politics, the environment, and religion. Most of the unchurched high school students K.J. talks to are politically liberal, and they consider the church a bastion of Republicanism. The students are concerned about the environment; they value natural beauty. When asked, "Who is God?" they're likely to respond by saying, "God is everywhere, in everyone."

In the face of this, K.J. warns youth pastors not to venture into this arena unless they're prepared to listen to ideas that are radically different from their own and to rationally defend their faith.

"ALWAYS BE PREPARED TO GIVE AN ANSWER TO EVERYONE WHO ASKS YOU TO GIVE THE REASON FOR THE HOPE THAT YOU HAVE. BUT DO THIS WITH GENTLENESS AND RESPECT."
—1 PETER 3:15b

REACH OUT TO CANCER PATIENTS

This church has found countless ways to help cancer patients and their families.

- ☑ APPEALS TO CHURCHED AND UNCHURCHED CANCER PATIENTS
- ☑ OFFERS MANY ON-RAMPS FOR SERVICE
- ☑ BUILDS AUTHENTIC RELATIONSHIPS
- ☑ PROVIDES PRACTICAL HELP IN A TIME OF CRISIS
- ☑ FILLS A GROWING NEED
- ☑ CAN BE DONE BY ANY SIZE CHURCH

THE EVOLUTION OF THE IDEA

In the fall of 1999, Tom Robinson dreamed of reaching out to people suffering with cancer. A member of Cannon United Methodist Church in Snellville, Georgia, Tom had witnessed firsthand the struggles a family faces as one of its members battles cancer. He had watched as his best friend lost his wife to breast cancer. Tom longed to start a ministry that would help with the daily necessities of life that can become so overwhelming during this kind of ordeal. Thus began the Cannon Cancer Ministry.

Today, the cancer ministry has approximately 230 volunteers who selflessly minister to the needs of cancer patients, or "care receivers" as the ministry refers to them. Among countless other services, these loving servants cook for the care receivers, clean for them, drive them to appointments, and—just as important—listen to them.

A CALL FROM GOD

"This ministry just keeps getting bigger and bigger," says Sara Bazemore, Cannon Cancer Ministry director since 2003. "God opens doors every time there's a need. I believe these are his plans and this ministry is his desire."

Sara began as a volunteer with the ministry in 1999. As a registered nurse, she had a professional interest in the outreach, but she also had a personal one. When her father had cancer, he was able to be at home, and she had learned firsthand the day-in, day-out struggles a family faces when one of its own battles the disease.

Then, in 2001, her mother was diagnosed with cancer and died three weeks later. Sara took a yearlong sabbatical from the ministry and may never have returned had it not been for God's insistent pursuit.

In December of 2002, Sara recalls, "God tapped me on the shoulder and said, 'You need to get back in leadership' " of the cancer ministry. "I fought it. He had to knock me on the head a few times. I'm here only because I heard God's call. But I can't begin to tell you the blessings I've received as a result."

THE HEART OF THE MINISTRY

Cannon Cancer Ministry desires to reflect the love of Jesus Christ. The ministry doesn't require any care receiver to attend its church or any other church. The volunteers simply try to show God's love by being faithful disciples and praying daily for healing and comfort. "We open our hearts to those who are suffering," she says. "We rejoice in good news; we hold a hand or share a hug when the news isn't good."

"We don't compromise the fact that we are Christians," Sara says. "But we assist those who are non-Christians as well. We try to be the face of God by being people of hope and compassion." Sara says the ministry meets each care receiver exactly where he or she is at that moment in life—a life with cancer.

> " WE ARE GOD'S INSTRUMENTS, PROVIDING LIGHT IN THE MIDST OF A DARKNESS CALLED CANCER. "
> —SARA BAZEMORE
> *Director*
> *Cannon Cancer Ministry*
> *Snellville, Georgia*

"Each case means so much to us," Sara says. "When you have an elderly couple, one spouse trying to care for the other with cancer, it can be so difficult and traumatic. Or another case that will bring you right to your knees is a case involving a child." The ministry has had only one such case in its history—and the child involved is in remission and doing wonderfully.

"Cancer can put such strain on families and marriages. During this time of uncertainty, pain, and fear, our goal is to meet the spiritual, emotional, physical (nonmedical), and informational needs of those with cancer," Sara explains. "We are able to go out and do what Jesus would do—help those who are sick."

KINDS OF CARE

The Cannon Cancer Ministry has provided countless home-cooked meals to care receivers and their families, working diligently to meet their different likes and dislikes. They have even provided different menus to a family, one for the kids and one for the adults. In one instance, the meal team provided meals for the husband of a gravely ill care receiver. When the son, who lived out of town, came to visit, he was amazed at his father's healthy appearance. "It's the meals the Cannon Cancer Ministry has been bringing. He eats so well," replied his sister.

In addition to providing meals, one of the most needed services the ministry provides is transportation to doctor appointments and treatments. In just two months recently, the transportation team made 75 trips. One 82-year-old care receiver with breast cancer had trouble stepping up into the SUV of one of the members of the transportation team. The driver offered to bring her smaller car the next time. When she pulled up in her Mercedes convertible, the elderly woman said, "Put the top back, and let's go!" So off they went to the radiation clinic with the top down and the heat on.

The ministry doesn't end with meals and transportation. One care receiver lived alone, and because of the extent of her cancer, was unable to put up a tree to celebrate Christmas. Cancer ministry volunteers not only placed a fully decorated Christmas tree in her den, they also gave her an Advent booklet and cleaned her house!

Another care receiver wanted very much to sit on his back porch in a screened-in room. Members of the home-care team lovingly repaired the porch so he could enjoy the room and outdoors before his death. One summer, says Sara, the ministry sent a family to Disney World for two days. The ministry has also built wheelchair ramps, removed flooded carpet, manicured lawns, helped with minor plumbing problems, and assisted with household moves.

COMPONENTS OF THE MINISTRY

There are four main components of the Cannon Cancer Ministry: the people who make up the ministry, the Prayer Bearer ministry, the Relay for Life, and cancer education and prevention.

The People

- **Care Receivers**—persons with cancer whom the ministry is dedicated to serving.
- **Clergy**—a clergyperson who is accountable for the ministry, offering support and spiritual guidance to the caregivers as well as the care receivers.
- **Ministry Leader**—a director or co-directors who oversee the entire ministry. The leader directs and problem solves with the assessor coordinator and team leaders.
- **Assessor Coordinator**—the initial point of contact for people seeking the ministry's help. The assessor coordinator also trains and works closely with the assessors.
- **Assessors**—loving individuals who "walk" with care receivers and their families during the patient's illness. They assess the needs of the care receivers and communicate those needs to the various ministry teams.
- **Team Leaders**—individuals who support, organize, assign, and direct team members.
- **Ministry Teams**—those who perform the work to meet the needs of the care receivers. (See page 51 for a list of the teams.)
- **Correspondence Secretary**—the person responsible for e-mailing updates, maintaining current team lists, and sending greeting cards.

The Prayer Bearer Ministry

Prayer Bearers are handmade stuffed bears that are tangible reminders of prayer. The bears are made by members of the congregation and given to care receivers, children at Children's Healthcare of Atlanta, Ronald McDonald Houses, and Lighthouse Ministries. At this writing, the ministry has given away more than 3,600 bears.

"The bears are prayed over twice before they leave the church," says Sara. "I know of one grown man who sat clutching his bear as he received his chemo infusion. The bears remind the care receivers that we're praying for them."

According to Sara, the bears were the brainchild of Carole Sheppard, a cancer survivor and a member of the Cannon congregation. A few years ago, before the Relay for Life, says Sara, "Carole felt she needed an idea for our booth at the relay," and she thought of this tangible way of showing care receivers they're being prayed for.

Relay for Life

The Relay for Life is a Gwinnett County, Georgia, event to celebrate those who have survived cancer and to raise money for cancer research. Cannon Church sponsors teams who enjoy fellowship as they raise money for a worthy cause.

Relay for Life

Relay for Life is the nationwide signature activity of the American Cancer Society. It raises money to fight cancer and raise awareness of cancer in the community. There are thousands of Relay for Life events each year across America. This event encourages families, schools, companies, hospitals, and community groups to create teams of eight to 15 people to take turns walking around a track all night to raise money.

The common theme of Relay for Life is to have members of teams continuously walking, running, or rolling around a track for 12 or 24 hours to honor those who are surviving cancer, those who have died from it, and the efforts of all who fight it. Participation is open to people of all ages, backgrounds, and abilities.

Cancer Education and Prevention

This facet of the ministry strives to educate the congregation about cancer and its prevention. The ministry gives individuals information to help them make healthy lifestyle choices and changes that will lead to better health and perhaps prevent cancer.

"Yes, we have great treatments, but we'll never conquer cancer without thinking preventively," says Sara. Diet and exercise are important, she says, as well as an awareness of hereditary factors. "We try to plant seeds about prevention. We have offered health tips on diet and exercise in our weekly newsletter to the congregation and have shared information from Emory University on prevention and treatment."

> **GOD IS CALLING THE CANCER MINISTRY TO EDUCATE OUR CONGREGATION IN THE PREVENTION AND TREATMENT OF CANCER.**
> —SARA BAZEMORE

FUNDING

Funding for the ministry is provided by individuals who have been affected by cancer, by care receivers who give in appreciation for the services they've received, and by a generous couple who felt moved to give after reading an article about the ministry in The Atlanta Journal-Constitution.

MAKEUP OF THE CANCER MINISTRY

In all, 14 teams make up the Cannon Cancer Ministry. Not all teams are needed for every care receiver situation, but all are available. In addition to the 14 teams, there are three administrative posts.

Administrative Posts

- **Clergy**—Members of the clergy are available to help answer care receivers' questions concerning important issues such as sin, salvation, prayer, the sacraments, death, and cremation. Clergy members also support assessors, ministry team leaders, and team members by being available to answer questions, discuss concerns, and offer guidance.
- **Director or Co-Director**—This person organizes, deploys, and supports the ministry teams, as well as updates the clergy team. He or she directs and solves problems with team leaders and oversees the ministry's budget and public relations with the congregation, community, doctors' offices, and treatment centers.
- **Assessor Coordinator**—This individual receives initial information about each care receiver and prayerfully considers the assignment of the assessor. He or she communicates with the clergy, directors, assessors, and team leaders. The assessor coordinator provides training for the assessors and makes occasional home visits with new assessors or when otherwise needed. He or she keeps written updates from assessors, adds new care receivers' names to the prayer list, and sends updates and reminders to assessors. The assessor coordinator supports

assessors and is alert for signs of stress or burnout, advising the director of the need for assessor debriefing.

Cancer Ministry Teams

- **Assessors**—have a compassionate heart for cancer sufferers. They pray daily for their care receivers and walk with them and their families during the illness. They evaluate the spiritual, physical, emotional, and informational needs of care receivers and communicate their needs to the appropriate team leaders. Assessors follow up with care receivers by phone weekly or as needed and document their interaction, updating the assessor coordinator every two to four weeks. They are self-aware individuals who know when they themselves need emotional and prayer support.
- **Meal Team**—provides home-cooked meals to care receivers and their families.
- **Transportation Team**—transports care receivers to doctor visits and treatments. Members of the team run errands when needed.
- **Home-Care Team**—provides day-to-day home care such as cutting the lawn, trimming shrubs, raking, and making minor home repairs.
- **Housecleaning Team**—after receiving information from an assessor, sees that the household cleaning needs of a care receiver are met.
- **SWAT Team**—an emergency prayer team consisting of approximately 15 people who immediately pray for care receivers whose conditions have worsened.
- **Communication Team**—communicates news about the cancer ministry to the congregation. Members of this team also distribute ministry brochures to doctors' offices, treatment clinics, and oncology offices.
- **Legal Team**—assists care receivers and their families with documents such as living wills and health powers of attorney.
- **Auto Team**—helps care receivers maintain their vehicles.
- **Resource/Reference Team**—refers care receivers and their families to specific community support programs and relevant governmental agencies.
- **Insurance Team**—helps care receivers and their families understand health care coverage and reporting requirements. The members of this team also help families communicate with insurance claims departments.
- **Cancer Awareness and Education Team**—provides assessors, care receivers, and their families with up-to-date cancer information.
- **Pet Care Team**—provides pet care and attention. Youth often help fill this need.
- **Funeral and Burial Team**—answers families' questions concerning funerals and burials and helps them make these arrangements.

MARKETING THE MINISTRY

Notices are put in the church bulletin periodically to let people know the ministry is in need of volunteers. "There have been times," says Sara, "when I needed assessors or members for the transportation team. God always provides."

Toward the start of the ministry, though, finding volunteers wasn't the problem—finding cancer patients was! "In the beginning, we had 350 volunteers, but we had no care receivers," says Sara. "We didn't understand the marketing aspect of the ministry."

So Sara and her staff created a brochure describing the ministry and what it has to offer. The brochure allowed the church to spread the word about the cancer ministry to oncologists and other doctors, radiation clinics, social workers, civic groups, school counselors, and other churches. They also shared the brochure with members of their own congregation. Since then, the number of care receivers has grown dramatically. Now care receivers even refer other cancer patients to the ministry.

"One of the most exciting things about the ministry is that former care receivers are now referring new care receivers," says Amy Morgan, associate pastor of Cannon Church. "One woman, whose husband died of cancer two years ago, not only referred her neighbor to our ministry, but has also organized her neighborhood to provide care on the days that the cancer ministry can't."

At this writing, the ministry has 15 care receivers. Most come from surrounding communities. The boundaries of the ministry, Sara says, are the five cities around their own city of Snellville. "We try to be sensitive to the distances our volunteers have to travel," says Sara. "If care receivers are outside our boundaries, we try to connect them with other churches."

LESSONS LEARNED

As the ministry has grown, volunteers have learned valuable lessons. For example, participants have learned to recognize the ministry's boundaries. This is especially important for assessors. "We can't play a medical role," says Sara, "but we can impact the other areas of a care receiver's life."

They've also learned that sometimes the most important thing a volunteer can do is listen. "We strive to love unconditionally," Sara says, "but we don't want to intrude." For example, she says, caregivers are encouraged to ask permission before praying with a care receiver and to respect the care receiver's response.

Respect for care receivers is an important element of the ministry. Care receivers tend to be proud, Sara says. "It's hard to ask for help. It's hard to have to rely on other people. We need to remember that."

The ministry has also learned the importance of educating people about habits that can lower their risks of getting cancer. "If a woman drinks several alcoholic beverages a day, that puts her at a higher risk of breast cancer," Sara says. "A lot of people don't know that." It's just that kind of information that Sara feels so passionate about disseminating. "There's a dire need for education."

RIPPLE EFFECTS

Not only do the care receivers benefit from the help, love, and compassion offered by the ministry volunteers, they may also gain a new awareness of who Christians really are. "I see those struggling with cancer gaining a better understanding about faith-based institutions and their desire to be of service," says Sara. "They realize we are genuine in our efforts to assist them."

Many times, Sara says, care receivers will say to her, "I didn't realize churches perform this kind of service. "What better way to represent Christianity!" Sara exclaims.

And the care receivers aren't the only ones who benefit from the ministry. "I see God doing wonderful things among those of us who are involved in the ministry itself," Sara comments. "Being part of the cancer ministry is a faith journey. We deepen our understanding of pain, anger, life, death, and grieving. To cope as caregivers, we have to be people of prayer. We have to depend on God to sustain us and guide us, as well as keep us emotionally stable as we encounter cancer at every stage."

"WHETHER THEY KNOW IT OR NOT, THEY SEE GOD TROUGH OUR ACTIONS."
—SARA BAZEMORE

So many times, Sara says, she's amazed at the Christ-like hearts of her volunteers. Stories get back to her about the flowers and cards they send, books they give to help care receivers understand specific cancers, groceries they buy, and personal-care items they provide. "They truly give unselfishly whenever they're called," she says.

LOOKING AHEAD

"Our call continues to be to serve those with cancer," Sara declares. The ministry is receiving more referrals and obtaining cases with increasingly significant needs.

To meet these needs, the church's board of trustees voted to use the house next to the church as a ministry house for the cancer ministry and Prayer Bearer ministry. The house has now been named the Hope House and will be home to a manufacturing floor for the Prayer Bearers, an office for the cancer ministry, and a library full of information about cancer. The vision is to one day provide a respite for caregivers by offering a day-care center for those with the disease.

The ministry is also being recognized outside the boundaries of Snellville, Georgia. "We have had increased media attention, more interest from the medical community, and educational support from the American Cancer Society," says Sara. In addition, there is "a desire by the Georgia Cancer Coalition for the ministry model to be shared with faith-based institutions across the state of Georgia."

To that end, Sara will be working on a pilot program with the Georgia Cancer Coalition. She'll be visiting other churches in Georgia, one per month for six months, to share the Cannon Cancer Ministry model with them.

"It's not me," says Sara. "God has been so amazing. Had I been keeping a journal of how God has worked in this ministry, it would be a best-seller. I just try to listen. I can't take the credit. I love what I'm doing, and I love that it honors the memory of my mom and dad."

CHAPTER FOUR
IMPLEMENTATION

HOW YOUR CHURCH CAN REACH OUT TO CANCER PATIENTS

If the idea of reaching out to those suffering with cancer appeals to you and your church, remember these four critical aspects of a successful cancer ministry:

1. A **clergyperson** who is accountable for the ministry and available to offer support and spiritual guidance to caregivers as well as care receivers.

2. A **director of the cancer ministry** who is passionate and prayerful on behalf of the ministry. He or she must have the time to lead, delegate, listen, organize, market, implement, and document the activities of the ministry. He or she must be available to team leaders and members and be accountable to the pastoral staff. He or she must maintain confidentiality in dealing with care receiver cases.

3. A **creative presentation** delivered to the congregation to obtain volunteers for leadership and ministry teams. In Cannon's case, Tom Robinson made the memorable presentation. He stood at the pulpit and asked the following people to stand: cancer survivors and people with a friend, family member, or neighbor who has or has had cancer. Then he asked them to sit.

Next he asked the following people to stand: anyone who could cook, mow grass, drive a car, or walk a dog. "The entire congregation was standing!" exclaims Sara. Tom concluded, "This tells me that everyone is affected by cancer to some degree and that everyone is capable of helping those with cancer."

He then directed those who felt called by God to sign up to be a part the Cannon Cancer Ministry. The sign-up sheets listed the teams and their responsibilities.

4. A **plan to market the ministry.** Your congregation is the first place to seek care receivers. Your church may have members who have cancer, or they may know people with the disease. Then contact people outside the church to build a network within the medical community. Create a brochure describing the ministry; it will be a valuable tool in building the network. Media coverage is another valuable way to let people know of your ministry.

STEPS TO TAKE

Here are some practical steps to take in starting your church's cancer ministry.

1. Recruit a core team of individuals interested in building a cancer ministry at your church. Make sure to include a clergyperson and a potential director.

2. Evaluate the ministry teams described in this chapter. With your core team, prioritize which team or teams seem the most viable for your resources. According to Sara, the busiest teams will be the transportation and meal teams. Home-care teams will be especially busy during the spring and summer.

> **❝OUR MINISTRY BEGAN WITH BABY STEPS AND GREW INTO WHAT IT IS TODAY. AS PEOPLE WITH VARYING GIFTS AND ABILITIES BECAME LEADERS, WE TRIED NEW METHODS, AND A STRUCTURE EVOLVED.❞**
> —SARA BAZEMORE

3. Consider forming a team to pray for the ministry, especially for those with cancer and the people who are helping to meet their needs.

> **WE ARE THE CARE-GIVERS, AND GOD IS THE CUREGIVER.**
> —SARA BAZEMORE

4. Don't be afraid to start small. Cannon's Cancer Ministry began with baby steps, and yours probably will, too. You may want to begin by serving cancer patients within your congregation before branching out to the community at large.

5. As you decide on leadership roles, take spiritual gifts into account, and place leaders accordingly.

6. Set realistic goals. "Be patient," says Sara. "As the ministry gains momentum, you can take larger steps. As the seeds grow and bear fruit, the dream will become a reality."

7. Create a brochure outlining what your ministry has to offer the congregation and community.

8. Create a tangible reminder of the prayer your ministry teams will be offering on behalf of care receivers. For Cannon Church, the Prayer Bearers are that reminder.

9. Creatively present your vision for a cancer ministry to your congregation. Be ready to plug volunteers into roles.

10. When you feel your ministry is sufficiently established, begin networking in the medical community to gain more care receivers. Distribute your brochure to medical offices, social workers, other churches, schools, and treatment centers.

11. Above all, trust God to bless your ministry.

"This may sound obvious," says Sara, "but churches have to realize this is God's ministry, and, for it to be a success, God has to be the most prominent member of the team. He does equip us in the most incredible ways. We are only the instruments he has put in place to carry out his plan. God bless you as you seek to be a blessing to those suffering with cancer."

"THE LORD IS MY STRENGTH AND SHIELD. I TRUST HIM WITH ALL MY HEART."
—PSALM 28:7, NEW LIVING TRANSLATION

REACH OUT TO FIREFIGHTERS

A tiny, fledgling church shows how to get involved in meaningful outreach right away, without spending a lot of money.

The firefighters of Station 27 in El Paso, Texas

- ☑ EASY TO IMPLEMENT
- ☑ CAN BE DONE BY ANY SIZE CHURCH
- ☑ BUILDS AUTHENTIC RELATIONSHIPS
- ☑ REQUIRES A LONG-TERM COMMITMENT

THE EVOLUTION OF THE IDEA

When Ed Sinke was considering planting a church in El Paso, Texas, he shared an office with Sam Faraone, a fire and police department chaplain and former pastor. Over time, they discussed how a church could make a difference in a community and how, if they just looked beyond the walls of the church, they could find many opportunities to serve and influence the community. These discussions led to an exploration of firefighters' unique needs. Ed discovered that there are lots of simple ways to reach out to this special group of people. For example, when Sam mentioned that firefighters have to buy their own food during their 24-hour shifts, Ed thought, "That may be policy, but I don't like it." He decided that if the church plant he was considering ever took root, its first outreach would be to firefighters.

In 2004, The Lord's House of Prayer was born. And sure enough, an outreach to firefighters quickly followed. First, Ed spent a couple of weeks talking to his congregation about the idea. The people loved the idea of *adopting* a fire station—being there on a regular basis over the long term—not just reaching out to firefighters from time to time.

Ed and Sam met with the captain of the fire station and explained what Ed's 15-member church wanted to do: They wanted to buy the firefighters' food staples, cook dinner for the firefighters once a month, and pray daily for each firefighter and his or her family. He was careful to explain that the church was motivated by a simple desire to honor the firefighters, not to evangelize.

The captain looked at Ed in amazement, saying, "I've been in the department for 23 years, and in that time no one has ever done this. Sometimes people have brought us Thanksgiving or Christmas dinner—which was great—but no one has ever committed to the long haul." He gave his permission, and the outreach by a 15-member church to an 18-member crew of firefighters began.

ESTABLISHING TRUST

The church began by obtaining a photo of each firefighter and creating prayer cards for each one. The prayer cards include the firefighter's name, rank, and position. Every day, members of the congregation pray for the firefighters pictured on their prayer cards. And whenever they hear a siren, they stop what they're doing and pray that God will keep them safe and give them wisdom, strength, and courage.

At the beginning of each month, the church buys the fire station's food staples at a cost of about $150 a month. And when they find a good price on a special item, such as a brisket, they buy that, too. The pastor includes this expense in the church's monthly budget, and the money is drawn from the offering.

Once a month, the church cooks a meal at the fire station for one of the three shifts, rotating shifts so that each is treated to at least one meal over a period of three months. Church members cook whatever the firefighters want. Recently, for example, the church provided an Italian meal, complete with homemade meatballs, baked ziti, and lasagna, all served on tables covered with checked tablecloths. Most church members come to these dinners, sharing in the food preparation and the fellowship. Some simply come and watch, enjoying the interaction between the firefighters and the church. One couple in the church decided independently to fix breakfast for one of the shifts. It was a natural response to relationships that have grown organically over time. Ed says, "These guys have become a part of our family."

Ed lives around the corner from the station and drops by once a week, bearing doughnuts, asking for a cup of coffee, and building relationships with each visit.

When the church noticed that the fire station's gas grill was "a disaster waiting to happen," they took up an offering and bought the best stainless steel gas grill they could find, complete with a deep fryer. They presented it to the station at Christmas, saying simply, "We're giving this to you because we care. Enjoy it!"

To celebrate its first anniversary, the church held a barbecue at a local park and invited the firefighters and their families. The church served roasted corn, hot dogs, and hamburgers and set up games for the children and adults. The firefighters, their families, and members of the church had a great time. They simply had fun together.

> **Outreach Tip**
>
> *Be sure to check your municipality's rules for giving gifts to its various departments. There must be no hint of bribery or the idea that the church will gain special favor as a result of its generosity.*

When the battalion chief, who is responsible for six stations, learned of the event, he said, "Hey! Why didn't you invite the rest of us?" So when its second anniversary rolled around, the church invited all six stations, hosting crews from each station every hour for six hours. One crew stayed past its designated time because it was having so much fun playing volleyball, relaxing, and laughing.

But establishing trust takes time, patience, and honesty. One firefighter, who described himself as "an agnostic, at best," asked Ed why the church was concentrating on the firefighters rather than donating its time and money to poor kids in nearby Juárez. Ed responded simply, "Because God told me to do this."

Another, a rough-edged motorcyclist, tried his best to rattle Ed with antagonistic questions, but Ed was never unnerved. (Perhaps his stint as a bouncer in a bar prepared him well!) Now the man has become Ed's good friend and is trying to tame his lifestyle, partly out of respect for Ed and his beliefs.

Over the past two years, even the most cynical firefighters have come to trust Ed and his church. Now the firefighters at that station call Ed Sinke their pastor, and some of them have attended services at The Lord's House of Prayer with their families. The church recently purchased a building downtown to serve as a ministry center, and the firefighters have offered to help with renovations on their days off—friends helping friends.

SHARING THE GOSPEL

Since adopting the fire station, Ed says, "We've been able to share the gospel on so many occasions." For example, once a lieutenant called Ed and asked him to come to the station to referee a theological debate between two of his men, a Christian and a non-Christian. Over the course of the discussion that day, all six firefighters and paramedics on duty heard the gospel at least twice.

On another occasion, a veteran of the force suffered a tragic personal loss as well as an emotionally trying professional call. Over the course of several months, he worked through these painful events with Ed. In the end, Ed said, "I got to walk with the man through the valley of discouragement, despair, and recovery. What a privilege!"

RIPPLE EFFECTS

Through these relationships, God has opened doors of influence that Ed and the church had never anticipated. Ed is now one of the chaplains of the entire El Paso Fire Department. In this capacity, he opens meetings of the city council. He was invited to pray with the captain, whose wife had just died of cancer.

And his little church, that began by adopting one fire station, has now adopted in prayer an entire battalion of six stations.

At this writing, Ed is working with a member of the fire department to establish a citywide program called Adopt-a-Station. This program would encourage churches and citizens' groups to do for the entire fire department what Ed's small church has done for one station. There are 35 fire stations in El Paso and over 400 churches. Ed says, "Imagine how we could bless these people!"

Recently one small citizens' group used its own funds and physical labor to landscape a new fire station. Ed says, "How much more could the *church* influence the community if we just go to these people with the desire to serve and honor them?" In fact, he envisions a "tsunami of kindness" spreading throughout the city. "If we are just kind to these people, God will open the doors. We don't have to force the gospel on them. If we show hearts full of kindness, as Jesus did, they'll come to us and say, 'Tell us about this God you know.'

"But it will happen only if we serve first."

LESSONS LEARNED

As they've gotten to know this special group of people, Ed and the members of his church have learned some important lessons.

First, they've learned not to pry. Firefighters are a tightly knit group. Like a family, they share a deep understanding of the unique issues they face, and they tend to address them among themselves.

Second, when members of the church can't find a response to the hard questions they're asked, they say so. When they began this outreach, they didn't fully understand the kind of trauma firefighters endure. Some of the stories church members have heard are devastating. In the face of brutal, gruesome, horrific events, they often don't have any answers. They've learned to say, "I don't have answers to all your questions, but I'm here, and I'm asking God to be with you."

Finally, they've learned to allow relationships to develop slowly and to go where they're naturally going to go. Ed urges Christians not to view evangelism as a function. It is, he says, nothing more than the act of building loving relationships. And it is through these relationships that people may come to know that they are radically loved by an amazing God who cares about them more than they could ever imagine. And if they don't respond to God, they discover that the Christians in their lives continue to love them anyway.

IMPLEMENTATION

HOW YOUR CHURCH CAN REACH OUT TO FIREFIGHTERS

If this idea resonates with you and your church, remember these principles as you develop your own outreach:

Principle 1—Respect firefighters' views, even though they may be quite different from your own.

Principle 2—Understand that firefighters process traumatic events among themselves.

Principle 3—Allow relationships to develop gradually and naturally over time.

Principle 4—Answer questions honestly. If you don't have an answer, say so.

STEPS TO TAKE

1. Discuss the idea with your congregation over a period of several weeks. Gauge interest, brainstorm specific ways to reach out to firefighters, and gain the congregation's commitment to follow through.

2. Identify at least one person whose heart beats for this particular outreach. Ask him or her to commit to stopping by the station at least once a week to be the church's primary contact with the firefighters and to "blowing the trumpet" for this outreach to the rest of the congregation.

3. Meet with the captain of the fire station to request permission to adopt that station. Clearly explain what your church would like to do. Be sure to emphasize that the church's motive is not to evangelize; it is to honor firefighters in an ongoing, consistent way.

4. After gaining the captain's approval, meet with the firefighters and explain the specific things you'd like

> **IF WE FOLLOW SOUND RELATIONSHIP PRINCIPLES, THERE'S NO DOOR GOD WON'T OPEN FOR US.**
> —ED SINKE
> *Pastor*
> *The Lord's*
> *House of Prayer*
> *El Paso, Texas*

to do to honor them. Make it very clear that you're not there to evangelize. Explain that if you're asked about your faith, you'll talk about it; otherwise, you won't bring it up.

5. Implement your church's specific ideas for honoring the firefighters in concrete ways, paying attention to the principles described on page 62.

Adapting This Idea to a Larger Church

Form outreach groups of 15 or fewer adults, and help each group find a fire station to adopt. Your church could conceivably adopt every fire station in your community!

FINAL THOUGHTS ABOUT... AWKWARDNESS

One of the biggest barriers to outreach is the fear of being placed in awkward situations. Ed Sinke offers this advice to Christians who fail to reach out because they fear awkwardness:

1. If you're an introvert and take the Great Commission seriously, you'd better get over the fear of moving outside your comfort zone. Don't allow your fears to prevent you from doing what you know you should do.

2. If you have a pure heart and have thought through what you want to do and why, most of the people you encounter will be open to it.

3. Bear in mind that those to whom you're reaching out also have fears. One of the biggest is that Christians will try to shove their beliefs down their throats. Communicate to them that you are there to respect and honor them and to meet them relationally, not to advance an agenda. You can approach people in the Spirit of the Lord and minister greatly without compromising your beliefs.

4. Remember that building relationships is always risky and that you might indeed be rejected occasionally. But if God has given you the desire to serve these people, he will also give you the grace to keep going.

"PREACH THE GOSPEL AT ALL TIMES, AND, WHEN NECESSARY, USE WORDS."
—SAINT FRANCIS OF ASSISI

CHAPTER SIX
REACH OUT TO TEACHERS

A coalition of 21 churches bridges the gap between churches and schools by encouraging teachers throughout an entire city.

- ☑ PROVIDES EASY ON-RAMPS FOR SERVICE
- ☑ BUILDS AUTHENTIC RELATIONSHIPS
- ☑ CAN BE DONE BY ANY SIZE CHURCH
- ☑ CAN TOUCH AN ENTIRE COMMUNITY
- ☑ STRENGTHENS RELATIONSHIPS AMONG CHURCHES

THE EVOLUTION OF THE IDEA

When several pastors in Omaha, Nebraska, started talking about their desire to reach out to the city in a way that would build relationships and present Christ in a fresh way, the topic of public schools quickly surfaced. Like most public school systems in America, Omaha's faces ever-increasing problems as well as mounting pressures to succeed.

Armed with little more than a heartfelt desire to help, three of these pastors met with the superintendent of Omaha's school district, which employs 7,000 people. The superintendent was open to the pastors' ideas when it became clear that they had no agenda beyond understanding the city's needs and helping to meet them.

The superintendent described some of the most pressing issues, especially in elementary schools, where 40 languages are spoken and more than 400 students are homeless. Some schools have a retention rate of only 30 percent—only one-third of the students who begin classes in the fall are still there at the end of the school year.

When the superintendent mentioned that teachers spend an average of $500 a year of their own money on supplies and necessities that parents can't provide, the pastors decided to focus their efforts on teachers—the unsung heroes of the public school system.

After a series of meetings, the superintendent opened the doors to the schools by calling 48 principals together and inviting the pastors to explain their intentions for the upcoming year. The principals were skeptical at first, but after the pastors shared their vision and made it clear that they harbored no ulterior motives, the principals enthusiastically invited them into their schools.

Then the pastors took their idea one step further: Why not join with other churches in Omaha to encourage and support as many teachers as possible? The pastors spread the word to other Omaha churches until 21 churches were on board. Thus was born Embrace Teachers, an

> **"EMBRACE TEACHERS IS AN INCREDIBLE OPPORTUNITY FOR OUR PEOPLE TO BEGIN TO TOUCH THE LIVES OF TEACHERS, WHO ARE MAKING THE DIFFERENCE IN MANY, MANY CHILDREN'S LIVES."**
> —TOM FRALEY
> *Pastor*
> *Trinity Interdenominational Church*
> *Omaha, Nebraska*

interchurch initiative that reached more than 1,500 teachers and their families in its first year alone.

HERE'S YOUR SCHOOL. MAKE IT HAPPEN!

The 21 churches divided the 48 schools among them, and each formed teams to carry out its part of the citywide initiative. After that, the success of the initiative depended entirely upon the creativity and generosity of the individual churches. The ideas started flowing, and before long teachers all over Omaha were being blessed.

One church prepared omelets for teachers before classes started in the morning. One, recognizing that teachers (and often their families) go without a good dinner on the evenings when parent-teacher conferences are held, prepared a chili supper for each teacher's family and packaged the meals for easy transport to the teachers' homes.

One principal asked his teachers for wish lists—items they longed to have in their classrooms—then gave the lists to the church. When the church surprised the teachers with tote bags full of the things they'd asked for, the teachers were thrilled. They received everything from crayons to a telescope to a new industrial coffee maker for the teachers lounge.

One individual bought a brand-new refrigerator to replace the rusted one the teachers had been using for years, and one church completely refurbished a teachers lounge with new couches and fresh paint.

At the end of the school year, the 21 churches celebrated the teachers of all 48 schools at an event at a local civic center. The churches provided an inspirational speaker—a former teacher of the year—and held drawings for vacations in Mexico and a new car (donated by a local car dealer). Throughout the school year and the end-of-the-year celebration, the message was clear that the churches' only motive was to bless and support the teachers of Omaha.

From the outset, the response from the schools as well as the churches was immediate and enthusiastic—a sure sign that the need was real. Accustomed to criticism and ever-increasing challenges to educate today's children, the teachers were deeply and effusively appreciative of all that the churches did for them. And for their part, the church members were delighted to find easy, tangible ways to serve their city. Like many Christians, they had longed to help but didn't know how.

Omaha's superintendent of schools, who teaches a graduate class on school law at the University of Nebraska, Omaha, recently stated that Embrace Teachers is a model for healthy cooperation between public schools and the church.

At this writing, Embrace Teachers is in its third year. The program is well recognized in the 48 schools it influences, and pastors can walk into these schools, be introduced by the principals to teachers and students, and find a warm welcome. The pastors remain in contact with the superintendent to ensure that their churches' interaction with the schools remains healthy and appropriate.

> **"OUR GOAL IS TO BLESS AND SUPPORT TEACHERS. ULTIMATELY, AS BELIEVERS, PART OF OUR CONVICTION AND OUR FAITH IS THAT THEY WILL COME TO KNOW CHRIST."**
> — IAN VICKERS
> *Director of Community Relations Christ Community Church Omaha, Nebraska*

SHARING THE GOSPEL

The purpose of Embrace Teachers is simply to encourage and support teachers through love and good deeds. In this process, trusting relationships have been formed. When teachers share their frustrations and worries, church members might ask how they can pray for the teachers. And when the Christians are asked about the source of their hope, they have an opportunity to share their faith. But they do so only when asked.

Once a team from one of the churches asked a principal how the church could pray for him and his school. He responded, "I don't know." The following week, they discovered that the principal had placed a box labeled "Prayer Requests" on his desk. He explained, "If teachers and kids have prayer requests, I encourage them to write them down and put them in this box. Then I'll give them to you at the end of each week."

As trust and relationships have deepened, teams from the churches have visited teachers who are hospitalized or facing family crises. These acts are natural outgrowths of the intentional relationship-building that is an integral part of Embrace Teachers.

RIPPLE EFFECTS

In addition to serving teachers and their families all over Omaha, this initiative has allowed many longtime church members to find their service niche for the first time. Embrace Teachers has mobilized hundreds of people in the church who have always had a heart for serving God and the city but had never known how until they discovered this outreach. In one church, for example, 50 percent of those who have volunteered to embrace teachers had never been involved in any kind of outreach before. Because the program offers so many ways to serve at varying levels of commitment, it appeals to people of all ages and demographics.

According to Ian Vickers, director of community relations at Christ Community Church, "People who never before have felt a part of God's kingdom and never knew how to connect with the community are discovering their own gifts and are finding ways to share the hope they have in Christ. That's tremendously exciting."

The initiative has also brought people from churches all over the city together, creating new friendships and deepening understanding and acceptance. As these Christians recognize that they're working together to build God's kingdom, denominational and other barriers have fallen away.

> **For me, the most exciting thing about Embrace Teachers has been watching the church become a bridge to the community rather than an island within it.**
> —Ian Vickers

Finally, Embrace Teachers has helped to break down barriers between the church and public schools. The two groups began by talking about the one thing they knew they had in common: their desire to prepare children for productive lives through education. With this one motive in mind, they were able to move forward. Through simple acts of love and kindness, the church is resuming its place as an integral part of public life in Omaha.

LESSONS LEARNED

Cast vision; then decentralize. Embrace Teachers began as a dream shared by a few pastors of different churches in Omaha. They realized that the dream would become a reality only if they cast their vision to their congregations and then moved the initiative to the grass-roots level within each church. The organizational structure was quickly decentralized, as each church identified a point person to head up the overall effort and formed a team of volunteers to support each school. The teams then dreamed of practical ways to bless the teachers and facilitated ways for the church at large to support their efforts.

Promise less; provide more. During the first year, the churches learned not to set expectations too high. They committed to three acts of kindness to the teachers in the schools they had adopted. Then, as the outreach gained momentum and the congregations discovered the joy of serving teachers, they delivered more. From the beginning they were determined not to disappoint the people they were pledged to serve.

Don't view this outreach as an avenue to church growth. Those pastors who joined this initiative expecting it to increase attendance were disappointed. And they missed the point. The point is to express appreciation for teachers through acts of kindness and love. It's all about building the Kingdom, not individual church attendance.

Find ways to sustain the momentum. Many churches involved in Embrace Teachers during its first year rekindle the vision for this outreach every summer before school resumes. They share success stories from the previous year. They find new ways to reach people in the pews who might still be uncomfortable venturing onto school property.

For example, before launching Embrace Teachers' second year, the people of Christ Community Church were invited to take part in a two-hour service project after services one August weekend. Participants formed 17 teams, and each team visited one of 17 sites, nine of which were schools adopted by Embrace Teachers. Each of these nine teams was greeted by the school's principal and shown around the school and its property. Then the teams went to work helping to prepare the facilities for the start of the school year. One team painted a map of the United States on a playground; another raked and mulched the landscaping; another painted playground equipment; another painted murals inside the school. It was an easy way for church members to begin to feel comfortable on school grounds and to get their feet wet in a service project.

Form covenants with other churches. The Omaha churches have learned to ask all the churches involved to commit to one fall-to-spring academic year and to deliver a minimum of three acts of kindness and one service project to each school within that period. This covenant relationship goes a long way toward ensuring that commitments are kept.

IT'S ALL ABOUT THE KINGDOM.

C H A P T E R   S I X
I M P L E M E N T A T I O N

HOW YOUR CHURCH CAN
REACH OUT TO TEACHERS

If this idea resonates with you and your church, remember these principles as you develop your own outreach:

Principle 1—Begin with prayer and make prayer an integral part of the outreach every step of the way.

Principle 2—Connect with the "church of your city"—the churches and leaders who have a heart for the city.

Principle 3—Pledge to be salt and light to your city, making Matthew 5:13-14 the cornerstone of your outreach.

Principle 4—Let love for the teachers be your motivation, not your need to do something.

Principle 5—Honor teachers and administration as the gatekeepers to the minds and hearts of the next generation.

Principle 6—Promise less; do more.

Principle 7—Sustain what you start by building relationships.

> **WHEN WE DO SOMETHING OUT OF *OUR* NEED, IT REALLY IS ABOUT *US*, BUT WHEN WE LOVE THE TEACHERS, IT'S REALLY ABOUT *THEM* AND MAKING A DIFFERENCE IN *THEIR* LIVES WITH THE LOVE OF CHRIST.**
> —JON TRINKLEIN
> *Pastor*
> *King of Kings*
> *Lutheran Church*
> *Omaha, Nebraska*

STEPS TO TAKE

Embrace Teachers Omaha has created an excellent step-by-step manual for implementing this outreach. It includes sample brochures, letters, and invitations; position descriptions and specific ways to fill those roles; discussion outlines for initial meetings with principals; specific ways to inform the congregation and recruit volunteers; ideas for decorations; and much, much more. To download a free copy of this handbook, visit www.group.com/outreach.asp and click on "Embrace Teachers Handbook."

The following is an outline of the steps to take in planning and implementing this outreach.

1. Form a central committee composed of key church leaders who have a heart for the city and its teachers.

2. Meet with the school district's most influential gatekeeper (probably the superintendent of schools) to describe your vision for embracing teachers and to obtain this person's blessing.

3. Ask the superintendent to identify the schools he or she feels would benefit most from the outreach and to invite the principals of those schools to an informational meeting.

> **Outreach Tip**
>
> *Omaha pastors presented each of the principals at the informational meeting with a basket containing a book on leadership by John Maxwell, gift certificates for coffee, and other tokens of appreciation. They showed a professionally produced video describing the importance of educators to children's lives and the churches' desire to bless and encourage teachers.*
>
> *Although some principals entered the meeting skeptical and wary, by the end of the meeting, they enthusiastically invited the churches into their schools.*
>
> *The pastors used the same video to recruit volunteers within their congregation and showed the video to the teachers at the beginning of the school year.*

4. At the informational meeting with the principals, describe your vision and the practical ways churches want to encourage and support the city's teachers.

5. Recruit other churches with a heart for the city and its teachers to participate in the outreach.

6. Meet with the pastors of all participating churches to recast the vision and divide the schools among the churches. Some larger churches may adopt several schools, while smaller ones may adopt as few as one. To expedite the process of assigning schools to churches, have a large map of the city on hand, with the schools marked with small flags. At this meeting, share program ideas and methods for implementing the outreach, and ask each pastor to sign a covenant committing each church to the outreach. You may view a sample covenant by logging on to www.group.com/outreach.asp. The covenant is on page 14 of the handbook.

7. Organize the outreach within your own church. Identify a point person to champion the entire initiative within your church and to communicate with the central committee. This point person will form a core leadership team to facilitate and oversee the effort.

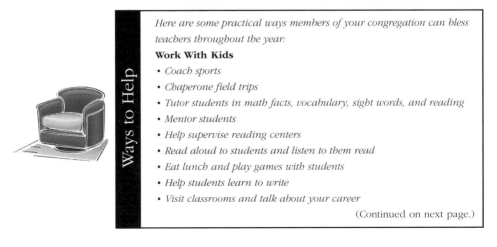

Core Leadership Team

Depending on the size of your church and the scope of its outreach, you may want to recruit volunteers to fill any or all of the following roles. All of these people would be accountable to the point person.

Prayer Leader—*a gifted leader who promotes, mobilizes, establishes, and oversees prayer for the teaching staff of the assigned school.*

School Liaison—*a leader who builds a relationship with the principal and facilitates communication between the church and school.*

Wish List Administrator—*a leader who coordinates the collection and distribution of items from teachers' wish lists and recruits volunteers from the congregation to assist teachers.*

Food Coordinator—*a leader who loves to be creative with foods and works with a team to bless teachers with treats and meals throughout the school year.*

Encouragement Writer—*a leader who organizes and leads a team that encourages teachers through personal notes and birthday cards written consistently throughout the school year.*

Arts and Crafts Leader—*a leader who loves to find creative craft ideas, create special projects, and lead a team to use these methods to bless teachers.*

For detailed descriptions of all of these roles, log on to www.group.com/ outreach.asp, click on the handbook, and scroll down to pages 21-46.

8. Plan a kickoff event for all of the teachers in each school before classes begin in the fall. Provide refreshments, such as a sheet cake and coffee, explain your church's vision for embracing teachers, and answer questions.

9. Solicit ideas from principals or the teachers themselves of specific ways to bless the teachers. For a sample wish list that could be distributed to teachers, log on to www.group.com/outreach.asp, click on the handbook, and scroll down to page 38.

10. Begin a drive at each church to collect the items requested by teachers.

11. Solicit volunteers to help with the outreach.

Ways to Help

Here are some practical ways members of your congregation can bless teachers throughout the year:

Work With Kids

• *Coach sports*

• *Chaperone field trips*

• *Tutor students in math facts, vocabulary, sight words, and reading*

• *Mentor students*

• *Help supervise reading centers*

• *Read aloud to students and listen to them read*

• *Eat lunch and play games with students*

• *Help students learn to write*

• *Visit classrooms and talk about your career*

(Continued on next page.)

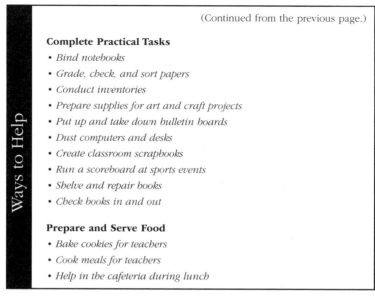

(Continued from the previous page.)

Ways to Help

Complete Practical Tasks
- *Bind notebooks*
- *Grade, check, and sort papers*
- *Conduct inventories*
- *Prepare supplies for art and craft projects*
- *Put up and take down bulletin boards*
- *Dust computers and desks*
- *Create classroom scrapbooks*
- *Run a scoreboard at sports events*
- *Shelve and repair books*
- *Check books in and out*

Prepare and Serve Food
- *Bake cookies for teachers*
- *Cook meals for teachers*
- *Help in the cafeteria during lunch*

12. Sometime in October, deliver the items the teachers have requested on their wish lists.

13. In November, January, and March, deliver some kind of treat to the teachers.

14. Recognize teachers in February with Valentine's Day cards.

15. Complete a service project benefiting the teachers in April.

16. Celebrate teachers at a citywide end-of-the-school-year celebration. (Teacher Appreciation Day is the first Tuesday in May, and Teacher Appreciation Week is the first week in May.)

17. In August, recast the vision for embracing teachers to the congregation and offer ways to involve more people in the outreach.

BUDGETING

The Omaha churches involved in Embrace Teachers have used a variety of methods for funding this outreach:

- Some churches include these funds in their annual budgets.

- Some ask the congregation for a special offering to fund the outreach.

- Some use the concept of an angel tree to solicit donations of material goods requested by teachers. (In this case, teachers' wishes are printed on cards, one wish per card. Participants from the church each choose a card, purchase the item named on the card, and return it to the church, where volunteers organize the gifts and deliver them to the appropriate recipients.)

- Some pair each school with a different ministry (small groups, Sunday school classes, college groups, and so on) within their congregations. Each group then decides how to fund the effort.

The important thing to remember is that, like most acts of kindness, the outreach doesn't require a great deal of money. Encourage your congregation to use its creativity to identify practical ways to bless teachers throughout the year.

Adapting This Idea to a Single Church of Any Size

The beauty of this outreach is that it can be done by a church of any size in any location. It doesn't matter if yours is a church of 50 or of 5,000; this outreach can be effective. A team of five people could adopt the teachers of one school and bless them throughout the year by tapping into the time and energies of the rest of the congregation. A congregation of 5,000, on the other hand, could bless the teachers of 10 or 20 schools by doing the same thing.

FINAL THOUGHTS ABOUT...
BUILDING POSITIVE RELATIONSHIPS WITH SCHOOLS

Embrace Teachers Omaha has put together these tips for working with schools and blessing their teachers and administrative staffs:

- Remember that you are not there to make more work for the staff. As you discuss ideas with the principal and other staff members, be sure to make this point clear. They will appreciate your sensitivity to their busy schedules. Carefully consider what it will take to make the activity work, and if extra people are needed, be sure to let the school know that you will recruit volunteers to help.

- Never proselytize staff or students. You are there to show appreciation for what teachers are doing for children in your community. Your witness should be a result of your actions, not your words.

- Listen carefully to the principal's suggestions and requests. You may have a great idea for an event, but the principal is the one who should determine what your team will be doing.

- Be patient when contacting schools. Principals are very busy, and it may take them a day or two to respond to your calls or e-mails.

"LET YOUR LIGHT SHINE BEFORE MEN, THAT THEY MAY SEE YOUR GOOD DEEDS AND PRAISE YOUR FATHER IN HEAVEN." —MATTHEW 5:16

REACH OUT
TO VISITORS

A youth group grows from 40 to over 300 by making
teenage visitors feel genuinely valued.

- ☑ BUILDS AUTHENTIC RELATIONSHIPS
- ☑ ALLOWS TEENAGERS TO TAKE OWNERSHIP OF A MINISTRY
- ☑ EASY TO IMPLEMENT
- ☑ CAN BE DONE BY A FEW VOLUNTEERS

THE EVOLUTION OF THE IDEA

In 1997, youth pastor Greg Spink had been at his job at Overland Park Church of Christ in Overland Park, Kansas, for about three years. He and his youth had *talked* a lot about ministering to others, but they hadn't *done* much. Finally, he challenged each of the 40 teenagers in his group to think of one outreach they would be passionate about pursuing if (a) they could lead it themselves and (b) they were guaranteed success. (Of course, success is never guaranteed, but Greg wanted the teenagers to dream big.)

One senior high girl said she wanted to find a way to make every teenage visitor to the church feel genuinely welcome and valued. The students started brainstorming and came up with the idea of personally delivering a gift to every teenager who visited the church, which at the time had an average weekly attendance of about 1,000 and was averaging 10 to 12 teenage visitors each week. They decided to take a bag of Hershey's Hugs chocolates to the home of each teenage visitor the Monday or Tuesday evening following the person's visit. As the outreach gained momentum, the church began providing mugs with its logo on them, and the students began delivering mugs filled with Hershey's Hugs along with a note saying, "You've been hugged and mugged by the youth of Overland Park Church of Christ."

From the beginning, the students established certain ground rules: First, because they dropped by unannounced, they made sure their visits were short, and they politely refused all invitations to come inside the homes they visited. They simply said, "We're from Overland Park Church of Christ, and we're here to thank you for visiting last Sunday and to tell you we hope you come again." Greg's business card was tucked in the mug along with a calendar of upcoming youth events. Visitors were encouraged to call if they had any questions.

Second, the outreach was a team effort that was organized and led by the teenagers themselves. At first, Greg and all the students who had agreed to participate piled into a 15-passenger church van and visited each home together. But over time, the teenagers organized themselves into teams, divided the number of visitors among them, and drove in their own cars. After six months, Greg rarely accompanied them. The outreach has been going strong ever since and is still considered the cornerstone of a thriving youth ministry at this church.

IT ALL STARTED ON A FRONT PORCH

According to Greg, as the outreach took off, "The youth group grew like crazy. So many kids landed at the church because kids showed up on their porches." During the next four years, in fact, the youth group grew from 40 to over 300 students from seventh through 12th grade.

Each team consisted of a junior high guy and girl and a senior high guy and girl. So if the person they were visiting was a senior high girl, for example, the senior high girl on the team did most of the talking on the porch. As a part of the visitation outreach, the team members also acted as greeters at church services and youth events. In this capacity, they kept an eye out for the students they had visited on their front porches. When they spied them, they reintroduced themselves, asked about their interests, and then introduced them to other students their own age with the same interests. If a guy played soccer, for example, the greeter might introduce him to someone in the youth group who was also a soccer player. These intentional contacts were instrumental in making visiting teenagers feel comfortable and eager to return. And the word spread. Students told friends at school about the church, and the word got out that this was a great place not only to make friends but also to take friends.

> **"BELONGING COMES BEFORE BELIEVING."**
> —GEORGE GALLUP JR.

SHARING THE GOSPEL

Greg remembers one front-porch visit with particular poignancy. The group, which happened to include Greg, showed up to deliver a gift to a senior high boy named Josh.* During the brief visit, they learned that Josh was from another state and was living in Kansas temporarily with his aunt and uncle. Two days later, Greg received a call from a counselor at a nearby high school. The counselor said, "Mr. Spink, one of your kids is here in my office, and he needs help. But we can't give him the kind of help he needs. I asked him if there is another adult he feels comfortable talking to, and he said you, his youth minister."

When Greg learned his name, he thought, "I met that guy one time on his front porch."

He drove to the high school and met with Josh, who told him his story. He said he was living with his aunt and uncle because his dad was an alcoholic and his mother had tried to commit suicide. Josh had found her during the attempt and had prevented her from killing herself. But she was so embarrassed and ashamed that she withdrew from Josh and would have nothing to do with

*not his real name

him. When he moved to Kansas, he knew no one his own age. His cousin, who occasionally visited Greg's church, took him to the church the first Sunday he was there, and the next day he was "hugged and mugged" by the visitation team.

Josh was lonely and lost and desperate for a friend. So right there, in the counselor's office of a public high school, Greg and he began to study the Bible together. They met once a week for a year. Josh made a faith commitment and later returned to his home state to meet with his father. He shared his faith with his dad, who also became a Christian and now leads an alcohol-recovery group. Josh is in college now, studying to be a youth pastor, and, according to Greg, "It all started on a front porch with someone saying, 'You matter to us.' "

RIPPLE EFFECTS

This outreach was conceived, organized, and led by teenagers, and this has been its greatest strength, according to Greg and the youth leaders who have followed him.

By taking ownership of the effort, teenagers have learned a lot about leadership. They've become attuned to ministry and what it takes to get things done. They've set high standards for the outreach, and every new team has risen to that standard each year. In addition, the outreach has helped teenagers discover their gifts and has provided opportunities for youth pastors to mentor the students leading the effort.

"DO NOT NEGLECT YOUR GIFT."
—1 TIMOTHY 4:14a

The outreach has also changed parents' perceptions of the youth group. They no longer consider it simply an opportunity for their children to have fun; rather, they've recognized that these students are doing something meaningful, are using their gifts, and are maturing spiritually as a result. In addition, the outreach has impressed the parents of the teenagers who are visited by youth group members. They are always pleasantly surprised to meet youth who have gone out of their way to make a face-to-face connection with their children.

Further, the outreach has built camaraderie between younger and older students. The two junior high students on each team benefit from the time they spend with two senior high students throughout the year, and the older students have risen to the challenge of being positive role models. It has also caused teenagers within the youth group to become better acquainted with one another. Because students involved in the visitation outreach intentionally connect returning visitors with teenagers in the youth group, they have to get to know many more people than they would otherwise.

Finally, the students involved in the outreach have a great time together. They often get together for pizza after completing their round of visits each week, and many have developed enduring friendships.

BRANCHING OUT

After establishing this outreach, the teenagers decided to begin a similar outreach to children who visit the church during vacation Bible school each summer. Total VBS attendance at this church averaged 450 children each year, and of those, 200 children were visitors. The youth volunteering at VBS formed five to seven teams, divided the visitors' address cards among them, and spread throughout the city to make each visiting child feel truly valued. Each year the teams visited about 50 children each night for five nights until all 200 had been personally thanked for attending VBS and encouraged to return.

LESSONS LEARNED

The students and youth ministers involved in this outreach have stuck with their original decision to **make each visit short and remain on the porch,** even when they're invited inside. This demonstrates respect for the privacy of the people being visited, as well as for their time. It also protects the students, as they are visiting strangers and are often in an unfamiliar part of town.

If a family isn't home, visitation teams leave the gift on the porch and then follow up with a personal phone call. While a bit less effective than a face-to-face visit, this still strengthens the connection between the visitor and the church.

Students leading this outreach have learned to require their teammates to **sign a commitment at the beginning of each school year** in which they agree to show up and to find a substitute when they can't. Each team has two alternates; it's up to the person who is unable to fulfill his or her commitment to line up a substitute.

To reduce the risk of auto accidents, only those high school juniors and seniors with good driving records are allowed to drive. Youth ministers repeatedly remind the youth that if there is even a hint of unsafe driving, the outreach will stop. And the students at Overland Park Church of

Christ have respected this unyielding rule. In the nine years the outreach has been in effect, there have been no car accidents.

Some years the level of commitment or the leadership abilities of the visitation teams aren't as strong as in other years. The youth pastors have learned to use these times to coach student leaders and help them discover their strengths and weaknesses. And the visitations have always been accomplished, so the outreach has always succeeded.

CHAPTER SEVEN
IMPLEMENTATION

HOW YOUR CHURCH CAN REACH OUT TO TEENAGE VISITORS

If this idea resonates with you and—just as important—with your youth group, remember these principles as you develop your own outreach:

Principle 1—The outreach must stem from a genuine desire to make newcomers feel valued and welcome.

Principle 2—The youth in the church must take ownership of the outreach.

Principle 3—The youth ministry staff should act as guides, not directors, in this outreach.

GENERAL STEPS TO TAKE

1. Before embarking on a student-led ministry, it's vital to do a lot of ground-work with your youth. In all that you do, stress the importance of balancing all areas of their faith, demonstrating that reaching out to others is as important as individual prayer and involvement in church activities.

2. Have ongoing, in-depth discussions about students' individual gifts.

3. Help teenagers discover their own ministry interests by challenging them to think of an outreach they would be passionate about pursuing.

4. Once they've identified a ministry objective, help them set ground rules. These should be designed to ensure their safety, few in number, and inflexible.

5. Act as a coach and guide as students organize and conduct the outreach on their own. Step in only when safety or the integrity of the outreach is compromised.

SPECIFIC STEPS TO TAKE

If your students decide to reach out to visiting teenagers, they might be interested in these organizational ideas from the youth of Overland Park Church of Christ (OPCC):

1. At the beginning of the school year, ask interested volunteers to commit to this outreach.

2. Form teams of four that can accomplish the necessary number of visits in two hours each week. Ideally, each team will consist of a junior high guy and girl and a senior high guy and girl. This will allow each visitor to be greeted by a person of the same gender and approximate age.

> **Outreach Tip**
>
> *The number of teams will depend on the size of your church, the anticipated number of teenage visitors each week, and the size of your town or city. For example, if your church averages three teenage visitors a week and you live in a metropolitan area, this outreach can be accomplished by one team of four. If you live in a fairly compact town, a team could probably visit five people in a two-hour period.*
>
> *At OPCC, the youth ministry staff decided to restrict the outreach to south Kansas City, as the metropolitan area is so spread out. Only those homes within a half-hour drive of the church were visited. The staff was strict about departure and return times; students were expected to return to the church within two hours so that they could be on their way home by 8 p.m.*

3. Identify two alternates per team. These are people who have expressed an interest in the outreach but aren't willing to commit to doing it every week during the school year.

4. Choose a student to lead the visitation team(s). This person will be responsible for the overall leadership and administrative aspects of the outreach.

5. In a written document, clearly define expectations of each person involved in the ministry. State where and when teams will meet, what they will be expected to do, and the duration of the commitment. For example, at OPCC, students meet each Monday from 6 p.m. to 8 p.m. throughout the school year, except during holiday weeks. In addition, they are responsible for greeting returning visitors at subsequent church services and youth events and connecting them with people with similar interests.

6. Obtain a signed commitment from each team member agreeing to the terms of the outreach and pledging to find a substitute whenever he or she is unable to participate.

Outreach Tip

The number of teenage visitors at your church will fluctuate each week. Regardless of the number of visitors from week to week, keep the number of visitation teams and the number of team members constant. For example, if you have three teams but only three visits to make, assign only one visit per team. With fewer visits to make, teams typically return to the church early or stop for a bite to eat together before returning to the church, building camaraderie and friendship.

At OPCC, when there are too few visitors for all of the teams to visit even one person, one or more teams visit a youth group member who has been absent from youth group for several weeks. They give the person a mug full of Hugs along with a note saying they've missed the person and encouraging him or her to return. This is a great opportunity for teenagers to find out if they've offended one of their members and to set about correcting problems. Often this gesture alone will be enough to cause a member to rejoin the group.

On the other hand, if the teenager doesn't return, the visit opens the door for an "exit interview"—an opportunity for a youth minister to find out why the youth no longer attends. This kind of interview can yield valuable information for the entire church staff.

7. Designate one high school junior or senior on each team to transport the team in his or her car each week. This person must have a good driving record and must maintain it throughout the outreach.

8. Decide how to pay for driving expenses. At OPCC, team members divide the cost of gasoline among themselves and reimburse the driver each week.

> To help ensure your students' safety, enlist the help of an insurance agent in your congregation. Obtain the driver's license numbers of all the students who are eligible to drive, and, with their permission, ask the agent to routinely check their driving records. If they receive more than one ticket in an 18-month period, disqualify them from driving as a part of this outreach.

Safety Tip

9. Inform the parents of each team member of the outreach and how it will operate. Obtain written permission for each person's participation.

10. Decide on a gift to leave with each visitor.

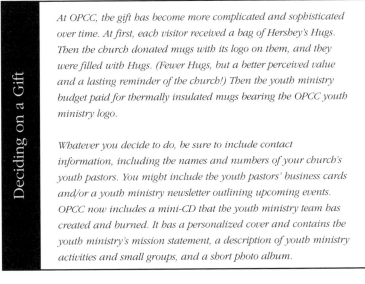

Deciding on a Gift

> At OPCC, the gift has become more complicated and sophisticated over time. At first, each visitor received a bag of Hershey's Hugs. Then the church donated mugs with its logo on them, and they were filled with Hugs. (Fewer Hugs, but a better perceived value and a lasting reminder of the church!) Then the youth ministry budget paid for thermally insulated mugs bearing the OPCC youth ministry logo.
>
> Whatever you decide to do, be sure to include contact information, including the names and numbers of your church's youth pastors. You might include the youth pastors' business cards and/or a youth ministry newsletter outlining upcoming events. OPCC now includes a mini-CD that the youth ministry team has created and burned. It has a personalized cover and contains the youth ministry's mission statement, a description of youth ministry activities and small groups, and a short photo album.

11. At OPCC, the team leader performs the following functions each week and works with a member of the youth ministry staff to resolve issues outside his or her purview.

- Monday afternoon, collect the visitor information cards filled out by teenagers at the previous day's service.

- Sort the addresses by geographical area.

- Prepare an itinerary for each visitation team, giving specific directions from the church to the first house to the second house, and so on, and finally back to the church. MapQuest is an excellent online resource for this purpose.

- Prepare the appropriate number of gifts, tucking contact information in with the gifts. (The youth pastor should ensure an ongoing supply of these items.)

- When visitation teams arrive at the church, hand out assignments, and with the teams, pray for their safety and for each person who will be visited.

- Check in with each team when it returns.

Safety Tip

After daylight-saving time ends in the fall, it becomes increasingly difficult to decipher house numbers. Consider supplying your visitation teams with strong flashlights to help them find the addresses they're looking for.

Adapting This Idea to a Smaller Church

This outreach can work in a church of any size in any geographical location. In fact, it would probably be easier to implement in a smaller town than a large metropolitan area, as students could visit more people in less time, and the cost of gas would be less. But as the youth at OPCC have proven, it can be done in a large, diverse metropolitan area. The key is that it stems from a passionate desire among the youth of your church to welcome others.

FINAL THOUGHTS ABOUT...INVOLVING YOUTH IN OUTREACH

Although Lettie Connolly, a former youth pastor at OPCC, loves how this outreach affects visitors, she especially loves what it does for the teenagers who undertake it. Through it, they began to understand ministry. They learn that church work isn't intimidating. And they learn the joy of serving. She says, "When young people experience how fun it is to bless others, their focus shifts. Their faith begins to grow legs. They develop a sense of purpose for their lives. They begin to understand their new identity in Christ. What a thrill it is to see these lights come on in the eyes of young people!"

REACH OUT TO PEOPLE WHOSE HOMES NEED REPAIR

A church blesses people who have spent
their lives blessing others.

- ☑ HELPS PEOPLE OF ALL AGES DISCOVER THE JOY OF SERVING
- ☑ TOUCHES THE HEARTS OF PEOPLE THROUGHOUT THE COMMUNITY
- ☑ PROVIDES MANY ON-RAMPS FOR SERVICE

THE EVOLUTION OF THE IDEA

Charity DeMott, 20, and her 19-year-old sister, Charisa, had lived in Honduras most of their lives with their missionary parents. When the time came for them to go to college, they decided to move into the home of their deceased grandmother in Moultrie, Georgia, a town of about 16,000. But the house had been vacant for years, and it was in a serious state of disrepair. Trees and shrubbery were so overgrown that the house wasn't even visible from the street. The ceiling in the living room was gone. The kitchen floor and cabinets had rotted, and the plumbing was shot. The electrical wiring was old and unsafe. In the bathroom, the walls and the floor beneath the tub had rotted away. The carpet throughout the house was filthy, and the walls were dirty and painted an ugly shade of green. The crawl space was full of trash. The roof was falling off the back porch, and the roof over the front porch had a gaping hole in it.

Charity and Charisa had spent most of their young lives blessing the people of Honduras. They had never had much in the way of material things. The people of Heritage Church in Moultrie had helped support the missionary work of Charity and Charisa's family for years. When they learned of the girls' plan to move into the house, they told them they would clean and paint the house, and the sisters were delighted.

But the people of Heritage Church planned to do much more than that. Leslie Peretti, the church's office manager and event and outreach coordinator, visited the site and assessed the damage. She went before the church and described all that would be needed to make the house livable. She asked the members of the church for their help. Then she went to business owners in the community and asked for their help as well.

Building contractors within the church of 600 volunteered their time, expertise, and materials to replace the kitchen cabinets and to repair the roof, ceilings, floors, plumbing, and electrical wiring. A furniture-store owner donated high-quality furniture for the entire house. Each of the five rooms was adopted by a small group within the church and completely outfitted with everything from pots and pans in the kitchen to towels and cotton swabs in the bathroom. One small group raised the funds necessary to buy a new washer, dryer, refrigerator, and stove. Trees and overgrown shrubbery were trimmed, and the house was repainted, inside and out.

The weekend before the house was turned over to the sisters, youth from Heritage Church and two or three other local churches landscaped the yard and walkways, installing new flowerbeds, planting bright flowers, placing mulch around trees, and mowing and raking the yard.

The result is a clean, safe, warm, dry, completely equipped home for two young women who have spent their lives blessing others but have never asked for help for themselves.

At 5:00 on a rainy Saturday afternoon, Charity and Charisa were scheduled to arrive. Students and adults who had worked on the house lined the walkways, standing under umbrellas, awaiting the girls' arrival. When the girls drove up, the crowd burst into cheers and applause. The sisters were stunned by the number of people who were there to show their love. The girls stepped onto the porch and were asked to turn and face the crowd as people from the church thanked them for all of their years of selfless service in Honduras and then presented them with the keys to their home.

When they stepped over the threshold, they were overwhelmed. Tears of joy streamed down their faces as they went from room to room, discovering all that had been done for them. On top of everything else, the church had left gift-wrapped presents in each room. According to Leslie, it's hard to tell who was happier that day, the recipients or the givers.

SHARING THE GOSPEL

When asked how the church decides who to help, Leslie responds, "We choose whoever needs help the most. The home-missions coordinator on our mission board keeps her eye out for deserving people in our community who really need help." For example, at the same time that Charity and Charisa's home was being renovated, Heritage Church was also renovating the home of an elderly black woman, Miss Daisy, who was raising her five grandchildren on a small income. Leslie Peretti likens Miss Daisy to the widow described in Luke 21:1-4: a woman who has almost nothing but gives everything she does have to help others.

As the exterior of her home was being painted, members of her primarily black neighborhood were intrigued to know why white people were working on Miss Daisy's house. When the workers said they had no motive other than to show God's love in a practical way, people were even more intrigued. Two boys in sixth and eighth grade asked if they could help paint the house. Soon they began attending the church. Now they have fallen in love with the church and are a part of its family.

Leslie says, "When we're asked why we do what we do, we reply, 'Because Jesus did the same thing.' That often leads to the question 'Who's Jesus?' From there, it's easy to say, 'Well, let's sit down and have a Coke and talk about it.' "

BUDGETING

Leslie's budget for both these homes was $1,000, and, incredible though it sounds, she came in $300 under budget. That's right—*under* budget. She says, "That's where God comes in! He moved the people in our church and our community to donate their time, energies, and material goods to this project. Without God's intervention in people's hearts, this idea would never have gotten off the ground, let alone soared."

RIPPLE EFFECTS

The single greatest side effect of this outreach has been to light a fire for service in the hearts of Christians. As they have blessed others, they've found that they themselves are even more deeply blessed. And they've begun to learn more about their gifts.

Once they've experienced the truth of Jesus' statement that it is more blessed to give than to receive, they've developed a passion for helping others, and that passion is contagious. As the church has grown, so has its level of volunteerism.

The outreach has also shown many people in the church that missions are not just for people in foreign lands; they are also for people in their own neighborhoods and communities. Changing their focus has helped them to see people in familiar settings with different eyes and has helped to break down social, economic, and racial barriers.

Finally, as with most outreach efforts, the act of working together to show God's love in practical ways has built community among the workers. Working alongside a relative stranger to re-roof a house builds a certain kind of camaraderie that frequently leads to a deep and lasting friendship.

LESSONS LEARNED

After three years, the people of Heritage Church have learned a lot of lessons about making this outreach successful. Here are some of the most important:

First, they've learned that **the point person who leads the outreach must be extremely organized** and detail-oriented.

At the same time, **this person's passion for the outreach must be contagious.** He or she must have the ability to inspire, recruit, manage, and encourage a wide variety of people before, during, and after the project.

Third, it is vital to **thoroughly assess what needs to be done** before going to the congregation and asking for help.

Fourth, when asking for volunteers and donations, **specifically communicate what needs to be done.** Ask who has each of the skills or materials required, and get a commitment for each item.

Fifth, **don't overlook the community at large.** Seek sympathetic business owners who may be willing to donate goods and services. Talk to local organizations and institutions to see if they'd be willing to help. For example, in renovating Charity and Charisa's house, students from Moultrie Technical College installed a new ceiling.

C H A P T E R   E I G H T
IMPLEMENTATION

HOW YOUR CHURCH CAN REACH OUT TO PEOPLE WHOSE HOMES NEED REPAIR

If this idea resonates with you and your church, remember these three simple principles as you develop your own outreach:

Principle 1—Select a deserving person or family whose need is the greatest. The recipient may or may not attend your church and may or may not be a Christian.

Principle 2—Always remember that actions speak louder than words.

Principle 3— The intention is to show people that you love and appreciate them and to demonstrate God's love in practical ways, with no hidden agendas.

START SMALL

This outreach didn't begin with a full-blown home makeover. Like most successful outreaches, its first initiative was fairly modest. The home of a single woman of very modest means was selected for improvement. This woman served at a local thrift store and rode a bicycle everywhere she went. Several weeks before the makeover, her bike was stolen. On the day the improvements were revealed (new exterior paint, shutters, landscaping, birdbath, and lawn furniture), the church also presented her with a brand-new red bike sporting a big red bow.

Any one of these gifts would probably have thrilled this woman. The church did what it could with the resources it had.

If yours is a small church, identify a project that your congregation can realistically complete, and, if possible, do the work over a longer period of time. As work progresses, the vision will catch on, and more and more people from the community will want to help.

STEPS TO TAKE

If you decide to help people whose homes need repair, here are specific things to do:

1. Ask God to help you identify a deserving person or family.

2. Interview the homeowner to learn his or her greatest needs.

3. Obtain the homeowner's permission to do the work.

4. Cast your vision for the outreach to the entire church.

5. Appoint someone with a passion for outreach to head up the effort. This point person should possess the gifts of administration, leadership, organization, and service. He or she should also be a gifted communicator and a good recruiter who can identify the right people for the right jobs. Once the point person has been selected, he or she will take the following steps:

   • Assess the home to determine the scope of the work, making a detailed list of everything that needs to be done.

   • Create a list of skills and materials that will be needed to complete every item on the list.

   • Go before the congregation to ask members to donate their gifts— prayers, time, expertise, labor, materials, and money—to the project. Distribute the list of the labor and materials needed to complete the work, and post a sign-up sheet for volunteers.

- Meet with local business owners to solicit needed items such as furniture, appliances, and services.

- Create a plan of action, detailing the order in which everything needs to be done.

- Create a master schedule, plugging in the names of the volunteers. Be sure to include people who have volunteered to help in supporting roles, such as running errands and providing meals, snacks, and beverages to the workers.

- Present workers with the schedule, and ask them if they can do the work at the scheduled times, juggling the schedule to meet the workers' needs when necessary.

- Begin work, coordinating the efforts of all the workers so that the appropriate jobs are done at the appropriate times. Be sure that the workers have what they need when they need it, including supplies, helpers, food, water, and encouragement.

- Assess progress at the end of each day, adjusting the schedule if necessary.

- If it's appropriate, plan a celebration for the homeowners, workers, and donors. (Be sensitive to individual personalities. Outgoing people may love a big celebration; others may prefer a more private unveiling.)

- The day before the house is turned over to the owners, inspect every detail and make last-minute changes if necessary.

- Deliver the keys to the homeowners!

- Send individual thank-you notes to everyone who helped; include a note of thanks in the church bulletin.

Scheduling Tips

In an outreach of this kind, coordinating everyone's work is vital because things must be done in a certain order. For example, in Charity and Charisa's home, the following tasks had to be completed in this order:

- *The property had to be thoroughly cleaned, inside and out. This included power washing and scraping the exterior in preparation for painting, roofing, and trimming overgrown shrubbery from around the foundation. In the cleaning process, problems that weren't readily apparent became obvious. For example, when workers scrubbed the area under the kitchen sink, a patch in the wall disintegrated, revealing faulty plumbing behind it.*

- *The ceiling was then repaired.*

- *As the ceiling was being repaired, the plumbing and interior electrical work proceeded, and the roof was repaired.*

(Continued on next page.)

(Continued from previous page.)

- *After the roof was repaired, the exterior was painted as the following steps were being taken inside:*
  - *The floors were repaired.*
  - *Holes and cracks in the walls were spackled and primed with a mold- and mildew-killing primer.*
  - *Kitchen cabinets were then installed.*
  - *Walls were painted.*
  - *Carpets were thoroughly cleaned.*
  - *Furniture was moved in.*
  - *Each room was outfitted with necessary items such as bed linens, dishes, and cleaning supplies.*
- *The landscaping was improved: Shrubs and trees were trimmed, new flowerbeds were made, walkways were repaired, and the lawn was mowed.*

FINAL THOUGHTS ABOUT...IGNITING THE PASSION TO SERVE

Leslie Peretti says, "Before I got involved in this outreach, I didn't know that I have a passion to serve others. But once I discovered the joy of service, I've come to realize that *everyone* has an innate desire to serve. The question for the church is 'How do we ignite this inborn desire?' I think the best way is to provide lots of on-ramps—even if a person only gives a cold bottle of water to a worker, that servant will be blessed and will want to reach out again, perhaps in a bit more meaningful way next time."

"BE CAREFUL NOT TO DO YOUR 'ACTS OF RIGHTEOUSNESS' BEFORE MEN, TO BE SEEN BY THEM. IF YOU DO, YOU WILL HAVE NO REWARD FROM YOUR FATHER IN HEAVEN."
—MATTHEW 6:1

CHAPTER NINE

REACH OUT TO THE HOMELESS

Churches throughout a community give homeless families a safe haven.

- ☑ ENABLES FAMILIES TO SERVE TOGETHER
- ☑ BREAKS DOWN STEREOTYPES
- ☑ PROVIDES EASY ON-RAMPS FOR SERVICE
- ☑ CAN BE DONE BY A FEW VOLUNTEERS
- ☑ INEXPENSIVE

THE EVOLUTION OF THE IDEA

For most Americans, the word *homeless* is associated with scruffy, bearded men standing on street corners holding signs saying "Will work for food." Most of us probably don't know any homeless people personally, and the idea that we ourselves could become homeless is almost inconceivable. But imagine what would happen if you or your spouse were laid off and couldn't find work for an extended period of time. Or imagine that you are one of the 41 million Americans who can't afford health insurance and one of your family members contracted a debilitating illness requiring a long hospital stay. How long could you continue to make your mortgage and utility payments as well as meet all of your other financial obligations? The reality is, many of us are only a few paychecks or one catastrophe removed from homelessness.

Karen Olson, a marketing executive from New Jersey, came to a similar realization one day in 1982 when she encountered a homeless woman in Grand Central Station. Rather than passing her by as she had done several times before, she stopped and gave the woman a sandwich. The woman responded by taking Karen's hand and beginning a conversation. Suddenly Karen realized that this was not a vagrant who couldn't or wouldn't work. This was a woman whose life had been turned upside down and who needed society's compassion and help.

USING WHAT'S AVAILABLE

After her first interpersonal encounter with a homeless person, Karen Olson and her two young sons did what was in their limited power to do: They began making sandwiches and handing them out to homeless people in New York City each week. As Karen learned more about homelessness, she also discovered that many people of faith yearned to help but didn't know how. And she began to realize that an infrastructure already exists to provide temporary shelter for the homeless: church buildings that stand nearly empty throughout the week.

So she started talking to congregations in her hometown, investigating social service agencies, and working with local businesses. Within 10 months, she had identified 11 churches that were willing to shelter homeless families on a rotating basis, engaged the YMCA to provide showers and a place where people could stay during the day, and found a local car dealer who was willing to discount the price of a van. In October 1986, the first Interfaith Hospitality Network was born.

At this writing, Interfaith Hospitality Network (now under an umbrella organization called Family Promise) comprises more than 100,000 volunteers and 10,000 congregations in 37 states. And it all began because one woman looked beyond stereotypes and saw a human face filled with desperation.

A SIMPLE, PRACTICAL IDEA

Here's how it works. A homeless family usually discovers IHN through a referring social service agency. In an initial interview, the local IHN director first ascertains if the caller is safe. If she is not safe or is being threatened, she and her family are referred to a safe house. When the immediate crisis is over, the family becomes a candidate for IHN's help. At that point, the director will want to know the family's current living status and what the parents' involvement has been in the life of each child. In this and subsequent interviews and through background checks, the interviewer is looking for a genuine family that has fallen on hard times—a family with a parent or parents who are willing to work hard to emerge from the devastation they face.

> **IHN DOES NOT INSTITUTIONALIZE SHELTER AS A SOLUTION TO HOMELESSNESS.**
> —FAMILY PROMISE,
> WWW.NIHN.ORG

After they've been accepted into the program, families spend their nights in local churches, where comfortable beds and hot meals await them each evening. During the day, school-age children go to school, while parents either work at jobs or spend the day at an IHN-sponsored day center, where they look after their preschoolers and pursue housing and employment opportunities. Because IHN has close working relationships with local social service agencies, it can direct families to sources of help that the families usually don't know exist. For example, the agencies might help parents find funding to allow them to get job-related training, or they might show them how to work with creditors to clear their credit records.

In a nutshell, Interfaith Hospitality Networks give distressed families time—time to take a deep breath in a safe, supportive environment. Time to assess their situations and find sources of help. Time to find work and begin to pay off debt. And ultimately, time to find homes of their own.

It's a simple idea that for the most part utilizes a community's existing resources and therefore doesn't require a protracted or expensive startup. IHN estimates that a network can be established in a community in 12 to 18 months and will cost about $70,000 in its first year. Altogether, IHN's cost of assisting homeless families is about one-third of that of public programs.

And it works. A family's average stay in an IHN is seven weeks, and over 70 percent of guest families find temporary or permanent housing before leaving.

ONE CHURCH'S INVOLVEMENT

To find out what this program looks like in the local church, we contacted Chris Perciante, ministries coordinator at Faith Evangelical Church in Loveland, Colorado. This church became involved because one of its members had heard about IHN and, after learning more, presented the idea to the church's board of elders for consideration—another instance in which one person's passion was the catalyst for a meaningful outreach by an entire church.

At Faith, the outreach is driven almost entirely by volunteers. One volunteer formed a team to oversee the ministry. After attending IHN training, the core team developed a simple manual for implementing the program, which has been in use ever since the church began its involvement with IHN in 2001. According to Chris, "The program was put together so well by IHN initially that we haven't had to make adjustments or reinvent the wheel from year to year. And it's so easy to implement that after a while, it becomes pretty automatic."

Once a year the church's representative meets with the local IHN director and other area churches' representatives to review the preceding year, share information, and be updated on emerging trends in the area's homeless population. The local IHN director is always available to support and consult with the churches, but IHN requires very little of the churches in the way of paperwork and reporting. This is not a bureaucracy-laden organization.

VOLUNTEERS

Faith hosts three to four IHN families for one week about four times a year. Four weeks before each visit, the church begins to recruit volunteers by announcing the need from the pulpit and posting a sign-up sheet on the all-church bulletin board. After doing this outreach for several years, recruitment is easy, according to Chris. "We can count on many of the same people to volunteer each time. It's usually just a matter of filling the gaps the weekend before the event by visiting adult Sunday school classes and asking for help in the few specific areas that remain unfilled."

At Chris' church, the outreach requires 35 to 40 volunteers to fill the following roles:

- **Setup**—These volunteers arrive at the church at 2:30 Sunday afternoon, remove the tables and chairs from the classrooms that will be used as the families' bedrooms, set up the cots that have been delivered by IHN, make the beds with church-supplied bed linens, place clean towels at the foot of each bed, and, if necessary, tape black plastic to the rooms' windows to ensure privacy. They post the families' names on the doors to their rooms. They move children's toys, a TV, and VCR into a common room along with couches, comfortable chairs, reading lamps, books, board games, and videos. Their goal is to make these rooms as welcoming and homelike as they can before the guests arrive at 5:00. These volunteers are usually finished setting up by 4:30.

- **Dinner**—Each evening of their stay, the IHN families arrive at the church at 5:00 in an IHN van. Volunteers from the church are waiting for them with a hot meal they've usually prepared at home and reheated at the church. Volunteers with children at home make this a family affair, involving their children as much as possible. They've found this interaction to be one of the most valuable parts of the program, even when their children are much younger or older than those of the IHN families. Older IHN children frequently bond with the young children of the volunteers and vice versa. But often the most special bonds that develop are between retirees and IHN children. Retirees can—at least temporarily—fill the need for grandparents that is universal among children. And the experience can be precious for both the children and the elderly.

  After dinner, volunteers and guests do the dishes and clean up the kitchen together. The volunteers remain with the guests until about 8:30, chatting with the parents, playing cards or board games with them, playing with the children, helping children with their homework—doing whatever they can to make the families feel comfortable and welcome. Sometimes the adults just want time alone and are grateful to be able to take a walk or go to their rooms for a while to read while the volunteers look after their children.

> **Outreach Tip**
>
> *It's a good idea to ask the volunteers providing meals to coordinate their menus. No one wants to eat lasagna three nights in a row!*

- **Overnight Hosts**—These folks—usually one person but sometimes a couple—arrive at the church at 8:15. Their job is simply to hang out with the families until everyone goes to bed around 10:00, ensuring the families' comfort, letting into the church those IHN parents who work late shifts, and responding to unforeseen situations such as medical emergencies. According to Chris, this is the one role that may take a little longer to fill, as people generally prefer to sleep at home in their own beds. At the same time, it's also the most fulfilling role, as the overnight hosts get to know the IHN families much more intimately than any of the other volunteers.

In the morning, the volunteer host prepares coffee and sets out breakfast and lunch items as parents shower and get their children ready for the day.

Recruiting Tip

Chris Perciante suggests that you begin your recruiting efforts by focusing on the position that is typically the hardest to fill: that of overnight hosts. Make a list of the people in your church who may be willing to take on this role and talk to them first. Always try to recruit one new person for this role, as it is usually the most meaningful and, of all the volunteer roles, brings the greatest joy.

- **Grocery Shopping**—The church recruits one person to shop for the breakfast, lunch, and snack items the church provides during the families' weeklong stay: juice, milk, cereal, bread, lunchmeat, cheese, microwave popcorn, and so forth. The church reimburses the volunteer for the cost of the groceries.

> **ALTHOUGH IT'S IMPOSSIBLE TO TURN A CHURCH INTO A HOME, WE DO AS MUCH AS WE CAN TO MAKE OUR GUESTS COMFORTABLE. SIMPLE THINGS—LIKE BEING ABLE TO GO TO THE REFRIGERATOR FOR A LATE-NIGHT SNACK—GO A LONG WAY TOWARD MAKING THE CHURCH A LITTLE MORE LIKE HOME.**
>
> —CHRIS PERCIANTE
> *Ministries Coordinator*
> *Faith Evangelical Church*
> *Loveland, Colorado*

- **Tear-Down**—The IHN families leave the church for the last time at 7:00 Sunday morning, one week after they first arrived. A team of volunteers arrives at 6:30 the same morning. This team is responsible for restoring the classrooms and common area to their Sunday functions before the congregation arrives. They vacuum the floors, return the furniture to its normal place, remove the black plastic from the windows, and so on. By 8:15, the church looks exactly as it did the Sunday before.

- **Laundry**—The Monday following the families' departure, two volunteers launder the bedding and towels used by IHN families. These items are the property of the church and are stored away until the church hosts another group of IHN families.

BUDGETING

Chris estimates that the initial financial outlay for this outreach was $500. This covered the cost of bedding, towels, and toys. Since beginning the outreach in 2001, the church has regularly received donations of all of these items as the original ones began to show wear. Now each time the church hosts IHN families, it spends about $100 a week—mostly for groceries—so it budgets $400 to $500 a year for this outreach.

SHARING THE GOSPEL

IHN families come from all walks of life. Many are recently divorced or never-married single moms. More and more of them are single dads. Some families have been financially and emotionally devastated by medical expenses. Some are grandparents who are caring for their grandchildren because their children are caught in the downward spiral of drug addiction. Some are churched; many aren't. Some are downright uncomfortable in church, any church. The key for Christians interacting with IHN families is to meet each individual where he or she is and to demonstrate love in practical ways, without evangelizing.

Even so, according to Chris Perciante, there are many opportunities for Christians to share their faith with IHN families. Many people in the program are intrigued by the outpouring of love shown to them and want to know the reasons for this behavior. In these instances, Chris says one way to draw them into a discussion of faith matters is to ask them what *they* believe—and to be truly interested in their responses. Beginning this kind of dialogue often opens the door for Christians to say, "Let me tell you why I think Christianity makes sense."

RIPPLE EFFECTS

Through this outreach, the people of Faith Evangelical Church have learned that homelessness is often not the fault of the homeless. Stereotypes have been shattered as the people of Faith Evangelical have come to know people in their own fairly affluent community who are homeless.

Instead of experiencing an overwhelming sense of futility when faced with such a pressing need, the people of Faith have become empowered. IHN's practical approach has given them a framework in which to tackle what otherwise seems an insurmountable social problem.

Even more important, in finding ways to help, they've discovered the joy of service. Some have become friends with those they've served and have remained in touch with them long after the families have re-established themselves in homes of their own. And it is through these long-term relationships that the love of Jesus has become real to many non-Christians.

LESSONS LEARNED

Chris Perciante offers these tips for anyone considering an outreach through IHN.

First, **encourage your members to be flexible.** For example, some IHN parents smoke. The idea of smoking on church grounds is anathema to many Christians, even if it is done outdoors. But it's important to bear in mind the stress these families are under; expecting adults who are addicted to nicotine to overcome this habit while dealing with homelessness is unrealistic.

Second, **accept the fact that some of these people may want nothing to do with Christianity.** The key is to show them Christ's love without preaching. Share your faith only when asked.

Third, **don't be offended if some people don't want to interact with you.** Imagine being in their situation—essentially acting as hosts to a new set of people every evening. Sometimes they understandably just need time alone. Looking after their children is one of the most appreciated gifts you can give them.

Finally, **treat all of the families fairly.** In one instance, Chris loaned a car to one man so that he could fill out housing applications at several locations around town. The other families felt he was given preferential treatment, and some resentment developed. Chris learned the importance of avoiding even the perception of favoritism.

C H A P T E R   N I N E
IMPLEMENTATION

HOW YOUR CHURCH CAN REACH OUT TO THE HOMELESS THROUGH IHN

If this idea resonates with you and your church, it's quite easy to become a part of an Interfaith Hospitality Network in your area. Log on to www.nihn.org to locate the IHN nearest to you.

If a network doesn't yet exist in your area, contact Family Promise to find out how one might be established.

Family Promise
71 Summit Ave.
Summit, NJ 07901
Telephone: (908) 273-1100
E-mail: info@familypromise.org
Web site: www.familypromise.org

FINAL THOUGHTS ABOUT...COMFORT ZONES

Kim Lockhart and her husband, Matt, had been looking for a way to reach out to their community when they were presented with the opportunity to serve IHN families an evening meal. Both have been church members for many years and have taught Sunday school and led small groups over the years. But they'd never been involved in any kind of meaningful outreach to the community.

Kim says, "When we were asked to prepare a meal for a homeless family, I thought, 'Well, that's a small enough thing. We can do that.' Even so, as the time drew near, I worried. I worried that we wouldn't have a lot in common with the homeless families, that we wouldn't have much to talk about. I worried that the atmosphere would be awkward, that a spirit of 'us vs. them' would pervade the evening. And I'm basically shy. I would prefer to spend my time in the background, in the kitchen, rather than striking up a conversation with a stranger."

Sound familiar? Most people, unless they're extraordinarily outgoing, share Kim's fears. But Kim wanted to move out of her comfort zone, and she wanted to set a good example for her two young children, Logan and Megan. So she focused on the visiting families instead of her fears and decided to do everything she could to make them feel welcome and valued.

Ultimately, she discovered that her fears were unfounded. "More than anything," she says, "I was surprised by how easy it was. Our kids alone gave us so much in common that barriers vanished right away." Kim and her family have served IHN families three or four times over the past year.

She says, "Our family is surrounded by Christians. My husband and I both work for Christian organizations, and most of our friends are Christians. All of the churches we've been involved in have been evangelistic but not intentionally socially conscious. We've always given our money to social causes but not our time, not our hearts. IHN gave us the opportunity to begin to do that. It was easy, convenient, and took very little of our time. This outreach has really shown me that Christians must be proactive in finding the lost because they're not going to seek us out. This is a good place to start."

"I WAS A STRANGER AND YOU INVITED ME IN."
—MATTHEW 25:35b

REACH OUT TO A WHOLE COMMUNITY

This church enables people of all ages and abilities to serve by providing accessible, just-show-up outreach projects on the first and third Saturdays of each month.

- ☑ APPEALS TO FIRST-TIME AS WELL AS SEASONED SERVANTS
- ☑ BUILDS LEADERSHIP ABILITIES
- ☑ FOSTERS SERVANT HEARTS
- ☑ CAN BE DONE BY ANY SIZE CHURCH

THE EVOLUTION OF THE IDEA

Where are you on Saturday mornings? If you're like many of us, you're enjoying your coffee at the breakfast table, luxuriating in a much-needed day off. Or you're taxiing kids to soccer practice or getting a jump on that list of errands.

But if you're a member of the United Methodist Church of the Resurrection in Leawood, Kansas, you might be putting the finishing touches on the lunch you'll serve at a local soup kitchen. Or you might be spending a few hours decorating cookies with kids at an urban children's home. You might even be providing companionship to an HIV patient. If you're a FaithWork volunteer, that is.

When Jonathan Bell came on staff in 2001 as the full-time director of missions, he found familiar terrain. "There were lots of people eager to serve, but it was difficult to get involved," he says. That all changed when the church began FaithWork—pre-arranged mission projects that virtually anyone can participate in on the first and third Saturdays of the month.

"Many times, mission or outreach ministries are not engaging in *hands-on* ministry," explains Jonathan. In some churches, for example, a committee handles grants and money raised for specific ministries, but the congregation is not involved beyond the monetary giving. In suburban churches in particular, he says, it can be intimidating to know where or how to serve outside your immediate community.

"We had mission ministries in place," says Jonathan. "We had helped build 65 Habitat for Humanity houses; we served a few meals during the holidays; we had mission trips—but the percentage of people involved was small." And for this church of 10,000, that just wasn't good enough.

So a group of volunteers visited Cincinnati's Vineyard Community Church, which practiced servant evangelism, doing random acts of kindness for others. The people in that church became known as servants, says Jonathan, because they were out there cleaning public restrooms, handing out cold sodas, helping people carry groceries to their cars—all with no strings attached.

> **WE WANTED TO EXPAND MINISTRY BEYOND THE WALLS OF THE CHURCH.**
> —JONATHAN BELL
> *Director of Missions*
> *United Methodist Church*
> *of the Resurrection*
> *Leawood, Kansas*

"We loved the model," says Jonathan. "We loved the regularity, the accessibility of the program. We loved that nothing was required in advance—you just had to show up." So he began thinking of how they could adapt the programs for their church in Kansas. "The nucleus," he says, "was that it had to be done on a regular basis, and nothing in advance could be required of the participants."

They could handle that.

THE FIRST SATURDAY

So on a Saturday in September 2001, the FaithWork mission program began. "We decided to start with one Saturday a month, so we showed a 20- to 30-second video about the program during the worship services," says Jonathan. "People showed up in droves. The response was phenomenal."

So phenomenal, in fact, that they went to two Saturdays a month in 2002. Today, they highlight the ministry in the weekly bulletin and on the Web (www.cor.org), plus it's featured as one of two or three portals for beginning to serve. "In fact, it's the foremost portal," says Jonathan.

Who shows up? Individuals, families with kids, students. "Our primary target is folks looking for a way to start serving," says Jonathan. "Initially, it was a lot of individuals, families, retirees, and students. Then the students brought their friends, and the families brought their neighbors. Within the last few years, we've been more intentional about including small groups."

Cathy Swirbul, FaithWork's director, has adjusted the program to enable small groups to serve together in FaithWork projects. She invites small groups to let her know ahead of time that they'd like to serve together. That way, she can make arrangements for them while still reserving projects for individuals.

THE HEART OF THE MINISTRY

The purpose of FaithWork, says Cathy Swirbul, is threefold. "First, it enables all ages to serve. There are various levels to dip into." Families with little kids and elderly folks can stay at the church and still be involved in missions. Others can serve in a nearby food pantry or soup kitchen. Still others can venture into urban areas to serve with one of the church's many partners in ministry. Each Saturday mission takes between one and three hours.

The second purpose, according to Cathy, is to allow small groups to serve together. Through outreach and discipleship, she says, small group members grow in their faith. "We serve people in need who can't pay us back, and this gives us a glimpse into God's heart."

The third purpose of the outreach, she says, is to "be our front door into missions." It's easy and well-organized

> **WE BECOME THE HANDS AND FEET OF CHRIST.**
> —CATHY SWIRBUL
> *FaithWork Director*
> *United Methodist Church*
> *of the Resurrection*
> *Leawood, Kansas*

and naturally propels people into mission involvement and leadership. For example, perhaps a participant serves one Saturday at a children's home. Moved by the experience, that person goes back on his or her own to visit again. "The outreach acts as a catalyst to get people started in mission ministry," declares Cathy.

Someone might start at FaithWork, she says, and come for a time. Then he or she could become a project leader, leading a team of volunteers in a soup kitchen and making sure that everything runs smoothly. Then that same person could get involved in greater mission ministries leadership.

"That's actually a big part of this program," says Cathy. The church offers mission leadership training two or three times a year for those who feel they'd like to grow in their mission work.

A TYPICAL SATURDAY

When people arrive on the first or third Saturday of each month, they have a variety of mission projects to choose from. Greeters stand at the door with menus of the day's projects. People simply sign up for the projects of their choice. After a short devotion, they gather with their project leader, coordinate directions and carpooling, and are off!

Typical projects include serving at a soup kitchen, visiting a nursing home or a children's home, or staying right at the church. "There are various levels of service," says Cathy, adding that a soup kitchen is a good introduction to missions. "Everyone can cook and serve food."

"We also partner with homes for neglected and abused children, where many of the kids are starved for attention. We do activities with them—crafts, reading books, decorating cookies, games—anything you'd do with your own kids."

Another example of one of the church's mission partners is the Hope Care Center, an inpatient treatment center for HIV-positive patients. "It's similar to a nursing home, where adults can learn how to deal with their disease," says Cathy. "One of our members is a nurse, and she encouraged us to reach out to this group. We do crafts, watch movies, maybe have a cookout. We want to show that we really care about the patients."

Participants who choose to stay at the church have lots of projects to choose from as well. It's not typical "church work," says Jonathan, such as picking up trash on the church grounds. It's strictly missions. "We might be making greeting cards for prisoners or making place mats or centerpieces for soup kitchens," he said. "We might be knitting baby hats and blankets to give to women's shelters or supporting outreach projects by making disaster-relief kits or bags for a community food drive."

Whatever project participants do, Jonathan stresses, the work is directed outside the walls of the church.

WHAT DOES A PROJECT LEADER DO?

In the beginning, Jonathan says, "We gave everyone a short evaluation form at the end of each project. The last question was always 'Would you be willing to lead?' That way, people self-selected to lead."

Now Cathy polls a random group of participants each week, rather than everyone. She generally chooses a couple of people per project and keeps a list of the people she has surveyed so she doesn't ask them twice. "She's always scouting for potential leaders," says Jonathan, asking leaders which volunteers they think have leadership potential.

On a FaithWork Saturday, the project leaders are expected to arrive early and be familiar with their projects. They pray with other leaders and Cathy before the doors open. Then they're available to answer questions as people arrive.

"After the devotion," Jonathan says, "the project leaders act as the point persons. They gather their participants, explain the project, and coordinate transportation and directions." At the site, they make the introduction to that ministry, then facilitate whatever it takes to get the job done. Before they leave, they pray for that ministry. Finally, they offer feedback to Cathy as follow-up.

Finding leaders hasn't been a problem, Jonathan says. "People find this ministry so inviting. It's a front door to service because it's flexible, accessible, and meaningful. If your heart is caught, you'll go back. And that becomes a steppingstone to leadership."

COORDINATING MINISTRY PROJECTS

"FaithWork allows us to be a transforming agent in the community," says Cathy, who coordinates all of the FaithWork ministry projects. She works with a half dozen or more urban partners. "It allows us to provide people and supplies that make a difference."

And when members of a FaithWork team arrive at a project destination, they come prepared. If they're serving at a soup kitchen, they bring the food. If it's a building project, they bring their own tools and supplies. "We come alongside our partners with supplies and funding. We have a budget. We send resources, not just volunteers."

Cathy makes the arrangements for FaithWork projects months in advance, matching a date with a project. "I'm always on the lookout for places to serve," she says.

SHARING THE GOSPEL

As she plans each effort, Cathy says, "We try to work with Christ-centered organizations whenever possible so the gospel can be shared."

A big part of the ministry, she says, is to share Christ when it's appropriate.

"There are a lot of opportunities." For example, when visiting a children's home, a group may read Bible stories or do simple VBS lessons with the kids.

Or take the example of the Hope Care Center, the HIV treatment facility mentioned earlier. "They were hesitant at first for us to come because we're a church," says Cathy. But just spending time with the residents on a regular basis let them know that church members were interested in blessing them individually.

After a FaithWork team held a cookout for the residents one Saturday, a young man e-mailed the church and asked if someone could come and tell him more about Jesus. "We said we could arrange that," laughs Cathy. "It was so powerful."

Cathy realized that there was a strong spiritual interest at the center, so she invited the residents to the church's Christmas Eve service. A few of them came, but they said it was difficult for most of the residents to come because of their health problems and compromised immune systems. Their volunteer coordinator asked if members of the church could hold a monthly worship service at the center. And they did.

At each service, says Cathy, the room is packed with residents. "They heartily participate in group prayer, sing their hearts out, and are very attentive to the message." The gospel is shared in some form during the message, she says, and they've given the residents an opportunity to silently commit their lives to following Christ. "Knowing how our gracious God works, I'm sure many of them have made that commitment in their hearts."

AN EFFECTIVE MINISTRY

When asked how many people FaithWork has reached, Cathy pauses. "Well, of our folks at the church, thousands. As for the people *they've* touched, it's hard to speculate. At one of our Christmas soup kitchens, 500 people attended! That gives you an idea."

On a typical Saturday, the ministry averages 150 volunteers. In November and December, the numbers go up to between 250 and 300. Also in November and December, each FaithWork Saturday offers 13 projects. That's a lot of people doing a lot of outreach!

"And on each Saturday, an average of 25 percent of the participants are first-timers," according to Jonathan Bell. "That's one of the measures of success I look for."

> WE TRUST THAT GOD WILL WORK THROUGH US. GOD'S IN THE BUSINESS OF REACHING PEOPLE.
> —CATHY SWIRBUL

Despite how successful FaithWork is, Jonathan strikes one cautionary note. At first, he says, some people had a tendency to think a few hours on a Saturday morning was what missions is all about. "We had to make sure people understood that this outreach is to be a steppingstone for deeper ministry in the community. It needs to go deeper than an occasional project."

CHAPTER TEN
IMPLEMENTATION

HOW YOUR CHURCH CAN START A SATURDAY MISSIONS MINISTRY

If the idea of providing an easy and accessible portal to missions resonates with you and your church, remember these principles as you develop your own outreach:

Principle 1—Start small and grow from there. But always aim outside the walls of your church.

Principle 2—Think broadly. You want this outreach to welcome everyone, from families with little kids to your senior folks.

Principle 3—Stay in contact. The more other churches and agencies you communicate with, the more opportunities you'll find for outreach.

Principle 4—See your ministry as a steppingstone to deeper outreach in your community.

STEPS TO TAKE

1. Read *Conspiracy of Kindness: A Refreshing Approach to Sharing the Love of Jesus With Others* by Steve Sjogren of the Cincinnati Vineyard Church (Vine Books, 2003). Think of ways to adapt the model to fit your church.

2. Network to create a list of partners in ministry. Visit lots of children's homes, soup kitchens, food pantries, nursing homes, and urban churches. Find Christ-centered organizations to step alongside in partnership.

3. Plan. You'll want to set up your projects a few months in advance. You'll also want to make sure that you provide regular opportunities for service, not a hit-or-miss program.

4. Provide various entry levels for participants. Include a variety of projects, including at least one mission project that can be done at your church (but not *for* your church).

> **IT'S NOT ROCKET SCIENCE. WE GOT LOTS OF IDEAS FROM OTHERS AND THEN ADAPTED THEM TO OUR OWN MINISTRY.**
> —JONATHAN BELL

5. Recruit project leaders. Get them excited about serving and leading.

6. Create a buzz in your congregation about the ministry. Show a short promotional video; create bulletin inserts and posters. Make sure to emphasize that the only thing participants have to do is show up!

7. If small groups wish to serve together, ask that they give you several weeks' notice so you can reserve other projects for individuals and families.

8. As participants arrive, have project menus readily availabledescribing the day's selection of mission opportunities. Have project leaders on hand to explain the details.

9. Look for potential leaders during each session. Provide a few leadership-training events throughout the year.

10. Keep detailed records. Track how many first-time participants you have in each session. Evaluate each project to see which are the most popular. Discover in which months of the year attendance is sparse or heavy, and plan accordingly.

11. Pray. Pray for more mission opportunities. Pray for your participants and leaders. Pray for the recipient ministries. Ask God to deepen the commitment of each person who serves. Thank God for the privilege of serving him.

> **THIS PROGRAM IS A FRONT DOOR TO MISSIONS. IT'S A CATALYST TO GET STARTED IN MISSION MINISTRY.**
> —CATHY SWIRBUL

IF YOURS IS A SMALL CHURCH...

Your church may not have thousands of members, and you may not start with a budget. Here are some ways to adapt the FaithWork model to a smaller church:

- Have volunteers bring their own equipment if the church can't afford to supply it. For example, if it's a sewing project for nursing home residents, participants could bring the thread and fabric.

- Use your church bulletin to advertise a supply drive. Be specific about what you need and when you need it.

- Ask local companies to donate a portion of the needed supplies or food.

- Use leftover supplies. For example, look for extra craft supplies after VBS, and then use those supplies to create crafts with kids at a children's home.

LIABILITY

According to Cathy Swirbul, if exposure to risk is a concern, a church could discuss the matter with its legal counsel. "We have minimized our risk by asking participants to drive themselves to projects and requiring that children under the age of 16 be accompanied by an adult. So far, liability hasn't been a problem."

FINAL THOUGHTS ABOUT...BEGINNING

Don't think you have to start out huge. "One of the first projects we did," says Jonathan, "was to hand out doughnuts to parents at soccer fields on Saturday mornings." Opportunities to serve are out there. Look for allies in the community, develop partner relationships, and start serving!

"DEAR CHILDREN, LET US NOT LOVE WITH WORDS OR TONGUE BUT WITH ACTIONS AND IN TRUTH."
—1 JOHN 3:18

CHAPTER ELEVEN

REACH OUT TO YOUR NEIGHBORHOOD

A man and wife single-handedly build a sense of community by reaching out to everyone in their neighborhood.

- ☑ APPEALS TO CHURCHED AND UNCHURCHED NEIGHBORS
- ☑ BUILDS AUTHENTIC RELATIONSHIPS
- ☑ CAN BE DONE BY ANY PERSON OR PEOPLE IN ANY SIZE CHURCH

THE EVOLUTION OF THE IDEA

The Neighborhood Outreach Ministry of Drue and Laura Warner began before they even moved into their neighborhood. As Laura explains, "My thinking on neighborhood ministry was really solidified after reading *Making Room for Life* by Randy Frazee. We read it as we were looking for a house to buy, and we had really been praying that God would lead us to the place he had prepared."

Drue adds, "We know we probably can't affect the entire city of Atlanta, but we may be able to impact our neighborhood and potentially even the suburb of Sugar Hill, where we live."

Laura and Drue say their hearts are in alignment with the ministry vision of their church, Perimeter Church, in Duluth, Georgia. According to Drue, the church's vision is "to bring the people of greater Atlanta and all the places we serve into a life-transforming encounter with the kingdom of God." He continues, "We believe that one of the greatest tools the church has today to accomplish such a mission is serving and loving others, particularly those with special physical or emotional needs."

As a result of that vision, Drue and Laura made a decision. "Since we're both extroverts and gifted with hospitality and mercy," explains Drue, "the best use of our time with the greatest potential for spiritual fruit in the lives of others is to focus our efforts on meeting, building relationships with, and serving our neighbors and local public elementary school."

THE HEART OF THE MINISTRY

The couple moved into Lenox Park, a neighborhood of 240 homes, in August 2004. They wasted no time in beginning their ministry. "Our first effort to begin meeting neighbors and building relationships was to coordinate a neighborhood food drive in October of 2004," says Drue.

It was important not to collect food door to door, but rather to have a central drop-off location. This gave neighbors the opportunity to stop by, have coffee and doughnuts, and meet one another. Drue and Laura also had a sign-up sheet available for neighbors who were interested in building a greater sense of community in the neighborhood. Ten people signed up.

After explaining their vision for community service and neighborhood relationships at the next homeowners' meeting, 15 more people signed up. And the ministry grew wings.

OTHER OUTREACH OPPORTUNITIES

The couple began hosting Saturday morning breakfast gatherings for neighbors who expressed interest in building a greater sense of community. At these breakfast gatherings, the group cast its vision for more outreach ideas, and Laura and Drue helped the group come up with ideas of how to implement its intentions.

The result? The neighborhood has held a tsunami-relief drive, a summer pool party, an Easter egg hunt, and a holiday decorating contest. In addition, 200 people attended a Halloween "meet and greet."

Drue even dressed up as Santa for the neighborhood kids! "I was asked to be Santa Claus for a Christmas party for foster and adopted children through Bethany Christian Services," he explains. "I figured while I had the suit, we could go ahead and use it as a relational ministry tool and invite neighborhood families to bring the kids over to our house to see Santa." In addition, Laura and "Santa" gave families a news article that directed them toward the spiritual significance of Christmas.

The couple also hosted a caroling party one year. They invited neighbors who had been involved in many of their other activities throughout the year, and almost 20 people participated. Laura says, "The group included retired people, young couples, singles, and families with kids. The diversity in age added a richness and sense of real community to the group, and that was a blessing."

A further blessing, she says, was the response to the caroling. The recipients, who Drue and Laura had carefully chosen, included a wife (with two children) whose husband had been killed in an accident the first week of that December, an elderly woman who had placed her husband with Alzheimer's disease in a nursing home the previous summer, a widow whose husband had died on Christmas day two years earlier, and several people who had just moved into the neighborhood.

"There was such a combination of tears and laughter along the way," recalls Laura. "We had a very rich, wonderful time together."

The newest outreach idea, as of this writing, is a campaign to read through the Bible. The couple also plans to open their home one Sunday night a month so people can come over to discuss spiritual issues. "We have no idea how this is going to go," says Laura. "But we feel that the time is right."

BUILDING RELATIONSHIPS

At this writing, Drue can readily count the ways that this Neighborhood Outreach Ministry has built solid relationships that might never have developed otherwise.

- Out of 240 homes, the Warners have built relationships with more than 75 neighbors and have developed close relationships with 20 of them.
- The neighborhood has donated more than 100 bags of groceries in the first two years of the ministry, building a firm sense of community among the donors.
- The Warners have identified deep emotional needs in four of their neighbors—needs that otherwise would never have been known.
- Four families have expressed interest in attending or have attended church with Drue and Laura.
- Two men have attended Perimeter's annual men's retreat.
- Laura and Drue have had conversations about spiritual issues with 12 families.
- Six to eight couples have expressed interest in starting a small group that would focus on marriage and family issues.

None of these things would have happened without the intentional outreach of Laura and Drue. "Think about our culture. At least in suburban Atlanta, we are very busy, scattered, disconnected people," says Laura. "When you get together with friends, it is typically to meet at a restaurant or go to some other activity. It is rare to spend time in someone else's home. But there the experience is much richer."

"WE VIEW OUR HOME AS A PRIMARY TOOL FOR MINISTRY."
—LAURA WARNER

SHARING THE GOSPEL

There are many ways to share the gospel, and certainly not all of those ways are oral. "We've shared the gospel through Christmas cards," says Drue, "and by including our neighbors in e-mails and prayer requests when we learned during Laura's pregnancy that our daughter had a heart defect."

Laura and Drue share the gospel by their actions more than their words. "We've been intentional about not verbally sharing our faith—that is, evangelizing—with our neighbors or inviting them to church events until we've built a foundation of trust and respect," explains Drue. "We don't want to be perceived as having an agenda of trying to convert them or get them to come to our church." After relationships have been forged, however, Drue says they are able to share the gospel freely because of the mutual trust they've established.

They strive to show their neighbors unconditional love and acceptance, rather than judging them. The couple wants to serve their neighbors with an attitude of humility, love, and acceptance.

Drue and Laura intentionally connect on a regular basis with other Christians they've met in the neighborhood. Together, they cast vision for the neighborhood outreach and pray together for their non-Christian neighbors.

Those efforts have paid great dividends. "I'd say that about 75 neighbors have experienced and/or heard the gospel through our neighborhood ministry," says Drue. "The relationships we're building will give us a great avenue for sharing the gospel—in our lives and in our words."

DAY-TO-DAY OUTREACH

Their neighborhood outreach hasn't cost Laura and Drue much in terms of dollars. "There's been a small financial cost to us," says Laura. "We often end up feeding others," she laughs. But since they piggyback on many of the events already planned and paid for within the subdivision, their costs are minimal, according to Drue.

Those events include pool parties, summer cookouts, and other social events planned and paid for by the homeowners' association. "We tap into those events," says Drue. "We make it a point to attend, meet new people, and deepen existing friendships."

"We make sure that we are volunteering, participating, and mingling with neighbors during these events," adds Laura.

Laura and Drue are intentional about giving their contact information to neighbors they meet for the first time. "We want them to have an opportunity to connect with us," explains Drue. "We typically don't ask for phone numbers, but we do try to find out where people live so we can stop by for a quick visit while out for an afternoon walk."

In addition, the couple serves the homeowners' association board as welcome team coordinators. The board sends them the names and addresses of people who have just moved into the neighborhood. "We try to make personal visits, delivering a current neighborhood newsletter and typically some cookies," Laura explains. Many of those first meetings result in further interaction, such as borrowing yard tools or asking for job contacts and school recommendations.

Other times, the couple invites new neighbors to dinner to meet established members of the neighborhood. "That way we're not the only contacts people have," Laura says. "We try to match newlyweds with other young couples, families with kids of the same age, and so on." At this writing, Laura and Drue plan to start a Saturday morning coffee gathering to which they'll invite both old and new neighbors.

THE COST OF THE CALLING

This outreach costs time more than anything else, but it's a cost both Laura and Drue are willing to pay. "We've installed a glass storm door, so the main front door is almost always open," explains Laura. "In fact, typically we close the main front door around 9 o'clock at night, and we joke about being closed for business."

All joking aside, the glass storm door serves a very practical purpose. "Many of our neighbors know that if the main door is open, meaning that you can see into the house and the porch light is on, visitors are welcome." Otherwise, she says, the family is enjoying personal time. "We tell people about our open-closed-door policy."

To preserve family time and avoid burnout, the couple generally keeps the door closed early in the morning as they enjoy breakfast together, and again in the evening during their daughter's bath and bedtime. In addition, Drue's responsibilities at the church often allow him to work at home half days on Fridays, during which time the door stays closed. The couple also values time away, making sure that family retreats are part of their annual calendar.

> **MANY OF OUR NEIGHBORS HAVE BECOME TRUE FRIENDS. IT'S NICE TO BE ABLE TO SEE THEM OFTEN AND NOT HAVE TO DRIVE AND BATTLE TRAFFIC.**
> — LAURA WARNER

The couple has built enough relationships with neighbors, says Laura, "that barely a day goes by that someone doesn't stop by for a short or long visit." Someone might stop by to borrow a spice; someone else might need a listening ear.

To make the ministry vital and viable, Drue and Laura have to be willing to surrender their time and to-do lists to be available to their neighbors. "Many Saturday projects get put on the back burner," says Laura, "not to mention the countless times I've just put the unfolded laundry back in the basket to make room for a neighbor on the sofa."

When household jobs simply have to be done, Laura says, "We'll talk to neighbors as we work—or invite them to join us! We just tell people we have to keep working when that's appropriate to the situation."

The ministry has also required a bit of personal sacrifice for the couple. In an intentional effort to spend more time at home, Laura hasn't been able to dive into all of the women's ministry activities she's interested in at church. "We've cut out other things in our schedule in order to spend more time with neighbors," agrees Drue, "things like taking time off from a church discipleship group in order to try to develop a group within our neighborhood." But both agree the extra effort is worthwhile.

"We want to be available to share our lives with the people God has placed around us," Laura says, "and that is key to this ministry."

BEARING FRUIT

Are Drue and Laura pleased with the fruit of this young ministry? Most definitely!

"In one way or another," says Drue, "this outreach has affected every neighbor (approximately 500 people) in our 240-home subdivision." If for no other reason, that impact has come about because Drue and Laura were instrumental in restarting the neighborhood newsletter. "Through communication comes influence," chuckles Drue.

> **PEOPLE ARE HUNGRY FOR A SENSE OF COMMUNITY, BUT NOBODY KNOWS WHAT TO DO. IT JUST TAKES SOMEBODY TO STAND UP AND SAY, 'LET'S DO SOMETHING!'**
> —DRUE WARNER

When asked to sum up their Neighborhood Outreach Ministry, Drue answers, "I would characterize this as a seed-planting, relationship-building, long-term ministry. Our goal is to be continually planting seeds of the love of Christ as we seek to establish and deepen relationships over the long haul."

The outreach has certainly been instrumental, says Drue, in building community both in his own church and in his neighborhood. "Our great passion," he says, "is to see followers of Jesus Christ who live within our own neighborhood begin to function as the body—not as members of various churches (while still maintaining active involvement there)—but as members of 'The Church of Lenox Park.' "

HOW PEOPLE IN YOUR CHURCH CAN REACH OUT TO THEIR NEIGHBORS

According to Drue, the idea of "loving your neighbor" is transferable from church to church, no matter what the size. "This model works best in subdivisions, dormitories, and condominium complexes," he says. "It's probably more challenging in a rural setting. However, there may be some great benefits in a rural setting because you'd have fewer neighbors and would be able to spend more time with them."

STEPS TO TAKE

If you'd like to help members of your church reach out to their neighbors, offer them this advice from Drue and Laura:

1. Pray. Ask God how he wants you to use your spiritual gifts, passions, and talents to minister to your neighbors.

2. Determine exactly who you will try to reach with the gospel. Set geographical boundaries—will you try to reach the people who live on your street? your block? your subdivision?

3. Brainstorm creative ways to connect with your neighbors. This can be as simple as delivering a plate of cookies to new neighbors or new parents.

4. Once you've connected with your neighbors, invite them to serve the community with you.

5. Rearrange your calendar so you can invest lots of time "in the field" (at home).

6. Be sure that all of your planning takes children into account. If their children aren't well-fed and cared for, single parents won't be drawn to this outreach.

7. Make service, love, and relationship-building your top priorities in dealing with your neighbors.

8. Wait for God's timing before you begin to verbalize your faith, all the while praying for God to open doors of opportunity and to be working in the hearts of your neighbors.

> **"PEOPLE DON'T NEED TO *GO* TO CHURCH TO *EXPERIENCE* THE CHURCH."**
> —DRUE WARNER

9. Be proactive in spending time with both Christian and non-Christian neighbors.

10. Discover which methods of communication seem acceptable (and unacceptable) within your neighborhood.

11. Invite and empower others in the neighborhood to get involved in the ministry.

12. Meet people exactly where they are before thinking of inviting them to attend a church function. Cautions Drue, "Motives can easily be misunderstood among non-Christians."

Planning a Food Drive

A neighborhood food drive is a good way to begin your Neighborhood Outreach Ministry. Here are several easy steps to take in organizing an effective food drive.

- *At least three weeks prior to the drive, get approval from your homeowners' association or apartment manager, if applicable.*
- *Two to three weeks before your drive, contact your local food bank to learn its needs and arrange a time to deliver your neighborhood's donations.*
- *One to two weeks before the drive, notify your neighbors of the plan, detailing the items needed, the date, and the time of the drive. Do this by distributing a letter to each neighbor within your established boundaries.*
- *One week before the drive, place yard signs throughout your neighborhood.*
- *On the day of the drive, set up a visible drop-off location in your neighborhood. You may want to use a tent. Supply coffee, doughnuts, and information about the organization that will be receiving the food.*
- *Provide a sign-up sheet to collect neighbors' contact information.*
- *Also ask neighbors to indicate if they'd be interested in future neighborhood outreach projects.*
- *Within one week of the drive, deliver the donations.*
- *Optional: After the drive, connect with neighbors who participated. Serve refreshments at your house or plan a cookout to say thanks.*

"LOVE YOUR NEIGHBOR AS YOURSELF."
—LEVITICUS 19:18b

REACH OUT TO LATCHKEY KIDS

A tiny church learns that its impact can be much greater than its size.

☑ BRIDGES GAPS BETWEEN RACIAL AND ETHNIC GROUPS
☑ CAN BE DONE BY A FEW VOLUNTEERS
☑ EASY TO IMPLEMENT
☑ INEXPENSIVE

THE EVOLUTION OF THE IDEA

Edison is a town of 1,100 in rural southwest Georgia. It is surrounded by the seven poorest counties in the state, and many people in Edison live below the poverty line. Approximately 60 percent of Edison's children are black, nearly 40 percent are white, and a small number are the children of Hispanic migrant workers.

One public high school in Edison serves the entire county of 5,000. But in the late '80s and early '90s, there was an exodus from the public school system. So many of the county's white high school students began attending a Christian academy 40 minutes from Edison that by 1996, the only white students left in the public high school were the very poorest who couldn't afford transportation to the academy. The remaining students were black and Hispanic. Race relations in Edison were so bad that the television news magazine *60 Minutes* profiled the town in one of its programs, which only served to inflame the situation.

At about this time, a group of about 20 Christians in Edison endured a painful split from the church some of them had been attending for decades. Without a pastor or a building, grieving over the split, Fellowship Baptist Church launched a search for a pastor. They found Stacey Simpson, in her last year of seminary at Candler School of Theology at Emory University in Atlanta. Although she hadn't intended to pastor a church, preferring a hospital chaplaincy, it was an instant match, and after earning her Master of Divinity degree, she moved to Edison in July 1996.

During Stacey's first year as its pastor, Fellowship Baptist concentrated on trying to heal. But sometime in 1997, the people realized they needed to discover their calling as a congregation, beyond being a sanctuary for people who had been hurt by the split.

Realizing that the church was not poised to grow in membership but did have potential to grow in its mission, members embarked on an intentional discernment process to discover that mission. They began a period of self-searching that included congregational discussion, prayer, fasting, and reflection.

A key component of this effort was discussion with people from the community who weren't members of the congregation. The church interviewed

20 community leaders, choosing a cross section of the community—blacks, whites, males, and females from a variety of professions and callings. They asked two questions: "What do you consider the most pressing problems in our community?" and "What do you think a church our size could or should be doing about them?"

After gathering this input, church members sifted through the information, looking for one or two ideas they had the energy and resources to pursue. The thoughts of one woman they'd interviewed, a former mayor and high school teacher, were especially compelling. She owned a trailer park on the outskirts of town. The residents were black, and many were welfare recipients. Many of the children didn't have anything to do after school or anyone to look after them in the afternoons. The children lived in a culture in which teenage pregnancy, drug abuse, and violence were commonplace. They desperately needed to be enfolded into a community of caring adults. The park's owner was sure that the 20 members of Fellowship Baptist could help.

ESTABLISHING TRUST

Accordingly, early in the summer of 1997, she invited all the residents and the members of the church to a cookout at the trailer park. This gave rise to a monthly cookout, which came to be called Summer Sundays. With no more equipment than a big grill, coolers, and a bonfire, the two groups came together once a month for a summer. The church's goal was simply to spend time with these families, getting to know them and learning how the church could minister to them. A lot of children and some adults showed up, and relationships began to form.

By the end of the summer, the church realized that the children needed a two- to three-hour after-school program. The church simply didn't have the resources for a five-day-a-week program, so it began a once-a-week initiative called Kids' Club.

On the last Summer Sunday of the year, the church distributed fliers describing Kids' Club to the trailer park residents and then began the program in the fall. Stacey and two volunteers went to the trailer park every Tuesday afternoon, offering a Bible story, related crafts, snacks, and games. During the two to three hours they were there, they learned about the children's week and about their lives. All ages were represented—from toddlers to a 21-year-old mother

"WHEN WE CAN'T DO AS MUCH AS IS NEEDED, IT'S EASY TO DO NOTHING. WE CAN BECOME PARALYZED BY THE SCOPE OF A PROBLEM. BUT WE LEARNED THAT EVEN THE LITTLE WE COULD DO COULD MAKE A DIFFERENCE."
—STACEY SIMPSON DUKE
Former Pastor
Fellowship Baptist Church
Edison, Georgia

of three. Usually 13 to 15 children showed up, but sometimes there were as many as 20 to 25. At times these three women were ministering to more people than were in their church!

From Kids' Club, two other initiatives grew. One was a children's Christmas party. Church members drove children to and from the party, and usually about 30 kids attended. Before Fellowship Baptist had a building of its own, the party was held in the office of one of the town's housing projects. Finally, after converting a downtown hardware store into a sanctuary, the church held its Christmas parties there.

In 1999, during the church's first summer in its new building, the church offered Summer Fest, its version of vacation Bible school. The volunteers selected a theme and planned Bible stories, snacks, games, crafts, and singing to support that theme. Again, members drove around town picking up children who wanted to attend. In 2000, Stacey's last summer at the church, 75 white, black, and Hispanic children attended Fellowship Baptist's Summer Fest. For Stacey and the members of her tiny congregation, it was the fulfillment of a dream that children of all races, ethnicities, and backgrounds could come together in one safe place to learn about Jesus.

In remembering that outreach, Stacey says, "It's not that we changed their world—girls still had babies at 17. But I still get letters from one of the unwed mothers who came to Summer Sundays. We didn't lift her out of her circumstances, but I know the fact that we cared had a positive effect on her."

RIPPLE EFFECTS

One of the most important byproducts of this outreach was its effect on the tiny congregation itself. Before reaching out to the community, the people of Fellowship Baptist were grieving the separation from their former church and all that entailed. This outreach quickened their healing as they began to sense the church's purpose. They realized that in addition to worship, Bible study, and fellowship, their church had a reason to exist. Filling a need in the community became critical to the church's purpose.

At the same time, Fellowship Baptist came to be known as the church to approach when no one else in the community would help. It gained a reputation as a church that would always try to do something to help people in need. It became known as an externally focused church, and in fact, was named one of 300 excellent Protestant congregations in a study funded by the Lilly Foundation. (See *Excellent Protestant Congregations: The Guide to Best Places and Practices* by Paul Wilkes [Westminster John Knox Press, 2001].)

Through this outreach to children, Fellowship Baptist established a sister church relationship with a black church in Edison. Together the two churches collected donations to establish a scholarship fund for a deserving high school student. In addition, the congregations worshipped and had lunch together once a year. The members of Fellowship Baptist began to learn how it feels to be a member of a minority group. It was a baby step toward racial healing in this small town where the racial divide is deep and wide.

Resource Tip

An excellent resource for church members yearning to move beyond the pews and into their communities is The Externally Focused Church *by Rick Rusaw and Eric Swanson (Group Publishing, 2004).*

LESSONS LEARNED

Through the process of defining their church's purpose and mission, Stacey and the members of Fellowship Baptist gleaned several insights that are valuable for all churches in the same situation.

First, they learned to **focus on ministry, not attendance numbers.** While all churches should do this, it is crucial for very small churches, as their survival may depend upon it.

Second, they decided to **do what they could with what they had.** Using the disciples as an example of a small group of people who made a big difference, they refused to be paralyzed by their smallness.

Third, rather than concentrating on what they thought they *should* be doing and what they *didn't* have, **they focused on what they had to offer and what they had the energy to address.** If they had tried to start a prison ministry, for example, it probably wouldn't have worked because this particular congregation didn't have the necessary energy or passion for that kind of outreach. They knew, however, that they could put some snacks together and visit children who needed the attention of caring adults. They were gifted to do that, and they had the energy to do it.

IMPLEMENTATION

HOW YOUR CHURCH CAN REACH OUT TO LATCHKEY KIDS

I f this idea resonates with you and your church, remember these principles as you develop your own outreach:

>*Principle 1*—You don't need specialists to show people that you love them. Some churches are able to develop specialized ministries, but that shouldn't stop others from doing what they can, without specialists, publicity, or professionally produced programs. Although we live in a culture that values slickness, churches of all sizes can still do basic things that Christians have always done to care for others. Offering overlooked children love through a Bible story, songs, snacks, crafts, games, and a time of sharing is a powerful outreach, regardless of how it's packaged.

>*Principle 2*—Whatever your setting, use the resources and connections you have. Although the owner of the trailer park was not a member of the church, she offered a place for the ministry to begin. It's unlikely that the ministry could have succeeded without tapping into that connection.

>*Principle 3*—Celebrate the good your church is doing. In many ways, this was a hard ministry for the people of Fellowship Baptist. Without regular encouragement, it would have been easy for them to burn out.

STEPS TO TAKE IN CHOOSING AN OUTREACH

1. As a church, enter into a period of self-study to discern your church's passions and gifts. Fellowship Baptist was guided by a book called *Discerning Your Congregation's Future: A Strategic and Spiritual Approach* by Roy M. Oswald and Robert E. Friedrich Jr. (Alban Institute, 1996). This

book provides practical tools to help a church complete a process that begins with spiritual discernment and continues through strategic planning.

2. Interview a cross section of your community. This step is critical. It will not only improve your church's understanding of the community and how the church is perceived within the community; it will also open doors to like-minded people with the resources to help.

3. Sift through the responses to your interviews. Identify the ideas that your church has the resources and passion to pursue. If yours is a small church, don't underestimate the power of choosing one thing and doing it well. Remember, you can't do everything, and you shouldn't feel compelled to try.

4. Cast a vision for the outreach to your congregation before, during, and after it's launched.

5. Find ways to encourage everyone involved in the outreach. Your enthusiasm will be contagious!

FINAL THOUGHTS ABOUT...BABY STEPS

When asked to relate a success story from this outreach, Stacey Simpson Duke graciously forwarded the following excerpt from "Perfect Foolishness," her sermon based on 1 Corinthians 1:18-31. It is printed here with the author's permission.

> The crucified Christ visited me one Friday afternoon in Edison, Georgia. I was standing in line at the dollar store downtown, minding my own business. Jesus was the last person I expected to show up.
>
> I was kind of down that day, having come from a pretty discouraging meeting with other folks who were trying to make a difference in our poverty-stricken county. Our little church's contribution to the effort was a kids' club ministry out at the trailer park. Once a week, we went out to the trailer park to tell Bible stories and play games, to sing songs and make crafts and have snacks. Mostly we went to let the children and their families know that someone loved and cared about them. Some days we felt pretty good about what we were doing. Most days we felt pretty disheartened. There were so many poor kids in our county and so many problems, and we were so few and able to do so little. We loved those children the best we could, but in the end we never really felt like our kids' club was a "success." We certainly weren't stemming the tide of poverty by singing songs and making crafts.
>
> I was thinking about these things as I stood in line at Bill's Dollar Store.
>
> The front door swung open, and a woman came through with her daughter. The little girl's name was Timinicia; she was a real live wire from

the kids' club, known for her toughness. She looked right at me and silently held up her hand in a small wave. No smile, no words. Just that little hand in the air. I smiled and called out to her, "How are you?" No answer. I said it again, "How are you?" She trailed off after her mother.

I felt like a fool. People were looking at me, probably wondering who I was talking to.

"Well," I thought, "at least she waved."

Then her older sister, 8-year-old Shontora, came through the door. She, too, looked right at me. I smiled and started to speak, but she disappeared before I could say anything. I not only felt like a fool, I became certain that I *was* a fool.

The next thing I knew, Shontora was right there at my side. Without a single word, she turned her brown eyes up toward mine and simply put her little arm around my waist. I said hello to her as she hugged me, but she never spoke. She just squeezed me tight and then walked away after her mother.

And in her simple action, the crucified Christ came to me and held my chin in his hand and looked me straight in the eye and said, "Keep losing your life. Just keep doing it. I know you feel like a fool. And you are. But that makes you an awful lot like me. So you just keep right on giving your life away every chance you get. Be my fool."

"THE PLACE GOD CALLS YOU TO IS WHERE YOUR DEEP GLADNESS AND THE WORLD'S DEEP HUNGER MEET."
—FREDERICK BUECHNER
WISHFUL THINKING:
A THEOLOGICAL ABC

CHAPTER THIRTEEN

REACH OUT
TO YOUNG READERS

This church's summer reading program has
been going strong for more than 15 years.

☑ PROVIDES EASY ON-RAMPS FOR SERVICE
☑ BUILDS AUTHENTIC RELATIONSHIPS
☑ CAN BE DONE BY ANY SIZE CHURCH
☑ EASY TO IMPLEMENT
☑ INEXPENSIVE

THE EVOLUTION OF THE IDEA

More than 15 years ago, a teacher preparing to retire worked with her church, her community's public library, and the local school district to begin a summer reading program in Alliance, Ohio. The program was so simple and filled such an important need that it has been going strong ever since.

One study after another has confirmed what all teachers know through experience: A child who is read to at an early age and who reads aloud throughout elementary school is far more likely to do well in school and in life. In his book *The Read-Aloud Handbook*, reading expert Jim Trelease cites a study of 155 fifth-graders. Those who read an average of 37 minutes a day outside of school scored in the 90th percentile on standardized tests. Those who read an average of 11 minutes a day scored in the 50th percentile, and those who read only one minute a day outside of class scored in the 10th percentile.

In a complicated world full of complicated problems, it's rare to be able to pinpoint such a simple case of cause and effect. And it's even more rare to be able to do something about it. Carol Ogline did just that.

First, she asked teachers from her school district to identify children who would benefit from a summer reading program. These are children who, because the habit of reading is not ingrained at home, lose ground each summer and eventually fall further and further behind in school. Next, she began to recruit adults to read with these children twice a week for six weeks throughout the summer. Finally, she coordinated her efforts with the local library, which had its own summer reading program. The result: Adopt-a-Reader, a program that has reached at least 1,000 children in this small town of 24,000.

STEP 1: RECRUITING

Several weeks before the end of the school year, Jill Greiner and Susie Buckel, teachers who currently spearhead Adopt-a-Reader as volunteers with Christ United Methodist Church, begin to recruit two groups: children in kindergarten through sixth grade who need reading time and adult volunteers who are willing to read with them. The program operates for six weeks each summer, with children and adults meeting at the church each Tuesday and Thursday from 9:30 until 10:45 a.m. The ideal child-to-adult ratio is one-to-one, and, according to Jill and Susie, recruiting the same number of each is the most challenging aspect of this program.

Teachers are the best recruiters of students. Before the end of the school year, Jill and Susie send teachers a packet of information describing the program and asking them to identify students who would benefit most from it. Several registration forms are also included; teachers are asked to send these home with the students they've identified along with a letter from Adopt-a-Reader inviting parents to enroll their children in the program. Jill and Susie also post fliers advertising the program in places such as the library and grocery stores.

The best recruiters of volunteers are the members of the congregation. The people of Christ United Methodist are asked to spread the word to friends in local service organizations, including high school and college organizations. As student registrations accumulate, Jill and Susie get a good idea of the number of volunteers they'll need. Over the years, the program has required as many as 100 adult volunteers and as few as 50.

At the same time, Jill and Susie work with the local library to ensure that Adopt-a-Reader augments and compliments the library's summer reading program. Each summer the library offers rewards for reading. The rewards may be based on the number of pages read, the number of books read, or the number of minutes or hours read. The time children spend in the Adopt-a-Reader program count toward the goals established by the library. The library also furnishes all of the books for the church's programs, delivering boxes and boxes of books, organized by age level, at the beginning of the summer.

In addition to readers, Jill and Susie recruit people to help administer the program. They include volunteers to help with safety and security, record-keeping, and snacks. Another small group of volunteers, who are unable to help during the week, spend an hour or so each weekend organizing the books and setting them out on tables.

Safety—At least two volunteers are needed to ensure the children's safety. One works in the parking lot, directing traffic and watching over the children as they move from the parking lot into the building and back. One is inside, checking children in and ensuring that they are released only to the people who are authorized to pick them up.

Record-Keeping—Jill and Susie keep track of children's attendance and the names of the volunteers who work with them in each session. The volunteers record children's progress toward their goals and make sure they're rewarded by the library—usually with stickers for reaching weekly goals and a book upon completion of the program.

Snacks—Four or five people volunteer to provide snacks for the children over the summer; on any given day of the program, three of them are at work in the church's kitchen. They provide healthy snacks such as fruit, apple juice, graham crackers, and milk. For some of the children in this economically depressed part of town, the snack may actually be breakfast.

The leader of this team buys the groceries each week and is reimbursed by the church's Christian Outreach Committee.

Setup and Cleanup—All of the volunteers help with setup and cleanup, and most invest a total of only an hour and a half each Tuesday and Thursday in the program from start to finish.

STEP 2: SCREENING AND TRAINING

Because they will be working with children, all volunteers must agree to undergo background and reference checks. The Sunday before the program begins, they also take part in "safe sanctuary" training, which includes a one-hour training video, through which they learn ground rules for appropriate interaction with the children in their care. They are told how to spot evidence of child abuse and how to report any cases of suspected abuse. Above all, they are trained to encourage children, never comparing their reading abilities with others' and always praising their efforts.

STEP 3: READING TIME

After children check in at 9:30 a.m., they're paired with an adult who has volunteered to read with them. Together they go to an area where books, sorted by age level, are displayed on tables, and the children select the books they want to read.

The pairs then move into the sanctuary and find comfortable places to read. The adult is there to read with the child, not to teach the child to read. Depending on the child's age and circumstances, this might mean that the child reads for a while, and then the adult reads a page or two. It might mean that the child reads all of the time and the adult helps only when the child is struggling with an unfamiliar word. Or it might mean that the adult does most of the reading and the child listens.

At some point during the hour-long session, children go to the kitchen for snacks. The timing of the snack is left to the adult volunteer's discretion. Sometimes children arrive at the church hungry, and it's clear that they can't concentrate until they've had something to eat. Volunteers are trained to be sensitive to these factors and to be flexible. The goal is to make children look forward to their time at the church, with adults, reading. The program is designed to make reading fun and interesting, something the children will be eager to do.

Altogether, the children and adults spend about 45 minutes actually reading together. At the end of this time, they log the number of pages or minutes they've read and are given any rewards they've earned through the summer reading program established by the library.

STEP 4: CELEBRATING

At the end of the six weeks, the church celebrates the children's achievements by inviting them and their families to a pizza party and special event such as a visit by a storyteller, a puppet show, or craft making. It's a fitting end to an effort that deserves to be celebrated and is always well attended by the children, their families, and the volunteers.

SHARING THE GOSPEL

The goal of this outreach is to help children improve their reading skills. This is done through kind, caring adults who consistently dedicate their time and energy to these children. In the process, children and adults build trusting relationships that may extend beyond the six weeks of Adopt-a-Reader. The Christian adults are acting as salt and light to these children whether or not they overtly share their faith. They reflect the love of Jesus by their very involvement in the program.

One little boy, for example, enrolled in Adopt-a-Reader for several years in a row and became attached to one of the volunteers. He's now in high school. Every Sunday, the volunteer and her family pick him up and take him to church with them. Through the summer reading program, this young man made a vital connection to a family of faith.

RIPPLE EFFE

Christ United Methodist Church is located in an economically depressed area toward the center of Alliance. Many of the children who take part in the summer reading program live in this area and have gotten to know one another through the program. They end up walking to and from the church together, forming friendships along the way. For many of them, this connection has become as important to them as the reading program.

Many of the children involved in Adopt-a-Reader are unchurched. Through this program, they become familiar with the inside of a church building and begin to feel comfortable there. They love looking at the church's stained-glass windows; they love sitting in the choir loft and the balcony; they love the sights and sounds of the sanctuary. What a great introduction to the idea of church as a place of comfort, nurturing, and learning!

Some students participate in the program for one summer; others return three or four times and build lasting relationships with the adults who have read with them. And some return as high school students to help younger children read, giving back some of the time and effort that adults gave them when they were small.

LESSONS LEARNED

In the 15 years of Adopt-a-Reader's existence, the organizers have learned some valuable lessons.

First, they've learned not to be afraid to **experiment with different approaches.** At the beginning of the program, for example, they offered two sessions every Tuesday and Thursday morning, thinking they could serve twice as many children with only half as many volunteers. Although the idea was good in theory, it actually proved to be an inefficient use of the volunteers' time. The organizers have learned to make adjustments every year to accommodate changing circumstances.

Second, because this program requires a lot of volunteers, the people at Christ United Methodist have learned to **tap into as many community organizations as possible.** And it's worked: Only about half of the volunteers are from the church. The others come from a wide range of community groups, and the volunteers range from 80-year-old retirees to high school students. This diversity has benefited the children.

Finally, they've learned to **trust God to fill needs.** While it's natural to fret over recruiting the right number of volunteers so that each child is matched with a reading partner, it's sometimes impossible. Requiring hard-and-fast commitments before admitting children to the program could eliminate this problem, but it would also prevent some children from participating. To avoid this, the organizers have chosen to trust God to fill the needs, and God hasn't failed them yet. Sometimes parents of children in the program volunteer when there is a need for last-minute help. Sometimes it's necessary for two or three children to read with one volunteer. In any case, the program has continued to work.

HOW YOUR CHURCH CAN REACH OUT TO YOUNG READERS

If this idea resonates with you and your church, remember these principles as you develop your own outreach:

Principle 1—The goal is to help children improve their reading skills, not to evangelize.

Principle 2—Be intentional about creating a safe environment. Conduct background and reference checks of all volunteers.

Principle 3—Be flexible enough to allow adult volunteers to be sensitive to each child's needs. Remember the overarching goal: to make reading pleasurable, to pique children's interest in books. A multitude of unyielding rules is unlikely to nurture this kind of interest.

STEPS TO TAKE

If your church decides to reach out to young readers through a summer reading program, here are specific steps to consider:

1. Meet with your local library and school district to learn about the programs that are currently in place to enhance children's reading skills. Identify a gap that your church can fill.

2. Discuss the need for a summer reading program with your congregation. To help convince your people of the vital importance of reading with children, check out the statistics cited in Jim Trelease's *Read-Aloud Handbook* (Penguin Books, 2001). This book also contains helpful tips for establishing a read-aloud program.

3. Identify a person in your congregation who is passionate about this idea, has the skills to spearhead the effort, and can take the following steps:

- Establish reading incentives, either independently or in conjunction with existing programs sponsored by the library, school district, or another entity.

- Several weeks before the end of the school year, prepare a packet for the elementary school teachers in your area. Include
  › a letter to teachers explaining the program, asking them to volunteer as summer readers and asking them to refer children who would most benefit from the program and to send registration forms home with those children;
  › at least six letters explaining the program to parents of referred children;
  › at least six registration forms for these parents to complete; and
  › a flier advertising the program and recruiting volunteers.

- Recruit volunteers by posting fliers on community bulletin boards, asking the people in your congregation to spread the word to people in the community organizations to which they belong, and taking advantage of whatever other advertising venues your community offers. For example, if the public schools in your community have a cable TV station, advertise there.

- In addition to recruiting volunteer readers, recruit people to help administer the program: people to ensure children's safety, to provide snacks, and to record children's progress.

- Establish a program to screen volunteers. Be sure to include a background and reference check.

> **Saftey Tip**
>
> *Part of good leadership is creating an environment that is safe for your church, your volunteers, and all they serve. We've included a risk-management assessment on pages 143-144 to help you identify your church's areas of strength and weakness and to serve as a guide to concerns that should be addressed. This assessment is one of hundreds of tools available through Church Volunteer Central, a Web-based resource that provides "innovative and effective resources for identifying, equipping, and releasing people into their gift-based ministries," including affordable, comprehensive background checks tailored to churches' unique needs. Check out CVC by logging on to www.churchvolunteercentral.com.*

- Establish a program to train volunteers. Be sure to stress the importance of encouraging young readers to feel good about themselves and their abilities. In fact, consider asking your volunteers to sign a pledge similar to Adopt-a-Reader's: "I pledge to be positive in supporting my reader. I will strive to encourage and respect the child. I will honor our relationship by refraining from discussing his or her abilities with others."

- During the program's first two or three sessions, have extra volunteers on hand to help register the children. Registration information should include the child's name, telephone number, address, school, completed grade, name(s) and contact information of the child's parent(s) or guardian(s), the names and contact information of the people authorized to drop the child off and pick him or her up, and food allergies.

- Match children with volunteers, ensuring that volunteers are at least five years older than the children they will be helping. Introduce parents to the volunteers who will be reading with their children. (Make sure the children and volunteers have name tags.)

- Direct children and volunteers to the tables containing age-appropriate books. Include a balance between fiction and nonfiction as well as light reading such as magazines and joke books. If your local library is not selecting the books, a good source of ideas for age-appropriate titles is *Honey for a Child's Heart* by Gladys Hunt (Zondervan, 2002).

- After children have selected their books and they and the volunteers have found spaces throughout the sanctuary in which to read, be sure that at least one person is responsible for ensuring they remain in plain sight throughout their time together.

- Have healthy snacks available in an appropriate part of the church building or grounds.

- As children check out, record the information necessary for children to earn rewards (names of the books, number of pages read, and number of minutes read, for example).

- Make sure children are rewarded as they attain benchmark achievements.

- Plan a party for parents, children, and volunteers to celebrate the children's successes. Adopt-a-Reader gives each child a small treat bag containing items such as bookmarks, puzzle books, bubble-blowing kits, and sidewalk chalk. Each item has a sticker with the church's name on it.

- After the program is over, meet with volunteers to discuss what worked and what didn't. It might be helpful to do this each week during the program's first year and less frequently as it becomes well established. Make adjustments as needed.

FINAL THOUGHTS ABOUT...PASSION

This outreach, like so many others profiled in this book, was sparked by the passion of a single person in a congregation. She recognized a profound need and knew that the church was in a position to help. To become an externally focused church, encourage your members to identify their passions, find solutions, and bring them before the church. It's amazing how much can be achieved as a result of the passion of one individual!

"THE SINGLE MOST IMPORTANT ACTIVITY FOR BUILDING
THE KNOWLEDGE REQUIRED FOR EVENTUAL SUCCESS
IN READING IS READING ALOUD TO CHILDREN."
—BECOMING A NATION OF READERS:
THE REPORT OF THE COMMISSION ON READING

Risk-Management Assessment

General Liability and Risk Management	Yes	No	?
Does our church have an ongoing risk management team?			
Do we have a policy and procedure manual for our volunteer program?			
Do we formally review the manual every year?			
Do we have general liability coverage for the volunteer program?			
Is one person responsible to review and update the liability coverage?			
Do we have events throughout the year that put us at greater risk for liability; if so, do we obtain coverage?			
Managing the Risks of Interviewing, Screening, and Terminating Volunteers	Yes	No	?
Do we have current ministry descriptions for each volunteer position in our church, including board members?			
Do volunteer ministry descriptions clearly indicate what qualifications are needed to fill each position?			
Do our ministry descriptions specify what physical requirements are required for the position?			
Do we protect ourselves against discrimination in the way we write our position descriptions?			
Do we complete a background check on volunteers?			
Do we regularly review performance with volunteers and document it?			
Do we tell volunteers in their initial orientation they'll have performance reviews? When? What will be covered?			
Do we immediately handle complaints or concerns about volunteers' behavior?			
Do we have written procedures for terminating volunteers?			
Do we provide volunteers with a written handbook regarding the policies and procedures?			
Do we clearly explain who will supervise volunteers and to whom they are responsible?			
Do we ask volunteers to sign a statement that they've received orientation and training and understand our expectations of them?			
Do volunteers understand the boundaries of their job descriptions; what they can and cannot do; where they should or should not be?			
Managing the Risk of Confidentiality	Yes	No	?
Do volunteers understand how our church defines confidentiality and privacy?			
Do volunteers understand what they can and cannot say?			
Do volunteers know the consequences of breaking confidentiality?			

(Continued on next page.)

(Continued from previous page.)

Managing the Risk of Personal Injury Liability	Yes	No	?
Do we explain safety procedures in working with people?			
Do we adequately post safety warnings for volunteers?			
Do we explain safety in their physical work space?			
Do we provide general safety training for volunteers?			
Do we have an incident report process for volunteers?			
Do we require volunteers to report any incident that is not consistent with routine activities?			
Do we abide by the Right to Know Act and provide information regarding it? (Contact the U.S. Environmental Protection Agency for information.)			
Managing the Risks of Volunteer Drivers	Yes	No	?
Do we have insurance that covers volunteer drivers?			
Do we have certificates of insurance on file for volunteers driving their own vehicles?			
Are volunteers made aware that they must notify us of any changes in their insurance policy?			
Do we need or have automobile insurance above and beyond the volunteer's own coverage?			
Are volunteers made aware that they may need to notify their personal auto insurance carrier of the volunteer driving activities?			
Do we check for a current, valid driver's license?			
Do we check driving records?			
Do we provide special driving training for volunteer drivers?			

C H A P T E R F O U R T E E N

REACH OUT TO DEVELOPMENTALLY CHALLENGED ADULTS

For more than 20 years, this church has been teaching developmentally challenged adults about Jesus.

- ☑ APPEALS TO CHURCHED AND UNCHURCHED ADULTS WHO ARE DEVELOPMENTALLY CHALLENGED
- ☑ BUILDS AUTHENTIC RELATIONSHIPS
- ☑ CAN BE DONE BY ANY SIZE CHURCH

THE EVOLUTION OF THE IDEA

In the spring of 1983, a couple in Buxmont Christian Church in Ivyland, Pennsylvania, posed an important question: "What can the church do for our son?" Their son, Jimmy, was a teenager with Down syndrome. Specifically, they wanted to know what the church could offer in terms of teaching their son about salvation. They wanted to know what the church could do to help Jimmy and his friends learn about heaven and that faith in Jesus is the only way to get there.

Two members of the church, Rick Fordyce and Dee Dee Schmalz, rose to the challenge. What *was* the church offering? Not enough to their liking.

So they invited a special education consultant to visit the church for a weekend and advise them on types of programs they could implement for Jimmy and his friends. Dee Dee, who at that time already had seven years' experience with the developmentally challenged community, spearheaded the program.

She and Rick couldn't find a church curriculum that suited their needs, so they created their own, adapting various Sunday school materials until they had what they hoped would be age-appropriate and engaging Christian education material for this special segment of their community.

Dee Dee coordinated the effort, recruiting and training a staff of four, and with between five and seven participants that first year, the Pug Wug ministry was launched.

THE PUG WUG MINISTRY

The Pug Wug Ministry at Buxmont Christian Church is self-funded, says Mike Kutler, current leader of the ministry. It's not funded by the church, although the church is solidly behind the outreach.

Mike's daughter, Tara, is a Pug Wug member, and that's how he came to know of the group. "The church that we had been attending had nothing for Tara, nothing to offer her. That's why we came to Buxmont. I started volunteering with the Pug Wugs, and we became members of the church. Then they asked me to take over the ministry, and I've been running it ever since." That was more than eight years ago.

Asked about the origin of the name of the ministry, Mike laughs and says, "No one seems to know. The ministry has been in effect so long, we've forgotten how it came to be called Pug Wugs!"

EVERY WEDNESDAY NIGHT

Buxmont's Pug Wug program follows a large group–small group model. The doors open at 7:30 p.m. as all the participants gather in the sanctuary. For the first 15 minutes of the program, the Pug Wugs enjoy a singalong and then a Bible story presentation.

"Sometimes we do a dramatic reading; sometimes we use puppets to tell the Bible story," says Mike. "We try to follow what the church is doing in Sunday school." Mike also takes prayer requests from the Pug Wugs in this large-group setting.

Then the Pug Wugs form three smaller groups. One group stays in the sanctuary for "church time." Another goes to a dancercise session, and the third group goes to an arts and crafts session. Each session lasts 20 minutes; then groups rotate so each gets to experience all three sessions.

During church time, Pug Wugs take turns praying aloud for the prayer requests they heard in the large-group opening time. They also participate in the Lord's Supper and give an offering.

At 8:45 p.m., everyone gathers again in a large group for snack time.

"We used to do four 15-minute sessions," says Mike, "but then we lost some staff and had to cut it to three classes a night. That actually worked out much better for us because it gave us more time in each session to really work with everyone."

APPRECIATING THE PUG WUGS

The ministry, made up primarily of adults with Down syndrome, is a blessing to everyone involved, says Mike. "I just love being with the Pug Wugs. That's the best part for me—being with these folks. Sometimes it's the little things that make a big difference."

For example, perhaps one of the Pug Wugs will come to a Wednesday night meeting in a bad mood. Maybe he or she won't want to socialize or participate. "But then we'll talk," says Mike. "I'll find out what's wrong, and we'll talk about it. Pretty soon, the Pug Wug is smiling and interacting. It makes me feel so good to have helped."

Parents, caregivers, and families of the Pug Wugs are also enthusiastic about the ministry, offering support and encouragement throughout the year to Mike and his wife. Parents are so enthusiastic, in fact, that they promote the ministry to other families. "Our growth has all been by word of mouth—parent to parent and Pug Wug to Pug Wug," says Mike.

The downside to that, he says, is the ministry currently can't accept any more participants. "We have a waiting list," says Mike. "I just hate to turn anyone away." At least another eight to 10 people would like to be Pug Wugs, but the church facility can't accommodate a larger ministry at this time.

> **"ROOM SIZE IS OUR BIGGEST LIMITATION."**
> —**MIKE KUTLER**
> *Director*
> *Pug Wug Ministry*
> *Buxmont Christian Church*
> *Ivyland, Pennsylvania*

SPECIAL EVENTS THROUGHOUT THE YEAR

In addition to their regular Wednesday-night gatherings, the Pug Wugs are treated to special events throughout the year. It's a busy schedule, but one that they enjoy.

In February, Mike and his staff host a Valentine's Day party for the group. They have special snacks and provide cards for the Pug Wugs to give one another. Also that month, the Pug Wugs are invited to attend a dance at a local Catholic church.

In April, instead of a regular meeting, Mike provides a game night, complete with bingo and special prizes.

In May, it's ice-cream sundaes all around. "They walk along the serving line and tell us which toppings they want," says Mike. "They love it!"

Come June, there are fireworks in the air. "There's a minor league baseball team, part of the Yankee organization, nearby. They're called the Trenton Thunder," says Mike. "We take the Pugs there to see fireworks every year. They really enjoy that."

Also in June, the Pug Wugs are invited to join in the fun at Buxmont's annual VBS program. Last year, about a third of the group attended VBS.

June is a big month, too, because the Pug Wugs have the opportunity to attend a Christian summer camp in Maryland for two nights. Last year, at least six members of the group went to camp.

"We break for the summer in July and August," explains Mike. "There are no regular meetings, but we stay in touch, so as not to go too long without seeing one another." In July, one of the church members hosts a swim party at her home for the Pug Wugs. "And in August, we all go to the Bucks County Playhouse to see a show. Last year, we saw *The Sound of Music*."

Then it's back to basics in September, with a hot dog night. In October, the Pug Wugs are invited to attend a Halloween dance at a local Elks Lodge. In 2005, they also went on a scenic train ride in historic New Hope, Pennsylvania.

In November, Mike and his staff host a fun night, featuring pizza, salad, dessert, and games. The group might also see another show at the playhouse.

In early December, a local Knights of Columbus group treats the Pug Wugs to a special Christmas luncheon and party. Later in the month, they have their own party at the church. The parents are invited, and there are presents for everyone.

"We used to do a secret Santa gift exchange, in which each Pug Wug drew another's name and bought that person a gift," says Mike. "But that didn't work so well. One person would get a coloring book, and another would get a gift costing $15. So we changed it and asked the parents to bring gifts for their own children. That way, they get just what they want."

ADMINISTRATION

The Pug Wug program began with five to seven Pug Wugs and four volunteer staff members. At this writing, there are 31 Pug Wugs, ranging in age from 18 to 61, with a waiting list of eight to 10. The current staff of nine, which includes Mike, is all still volunteers. A healthy ratio of Pug Wugs to volunteers is five to one, he says. The staff could accommodate more Pug Wugs, but the building can't.

Since the program is self-funded, the parents help out quite a bit. "We ask for a yearly donation of $30 for each Pug Wug," he says. "And we also take a weekly collection. The parents are really very supportive."

As for training, "It's basically one-on-one, hands-on training," says Mike. "We just take new volunteers around with us for a few weeks and show them what we do. When they're comfortable, they can lead a session. It's not hard to catch on." Some of the volunteers are members of the church, he says, and some are not.

> **SEEING THE JOY ON THE FACES OF THE PUG WUGS DURING WORSHIP PUTS ME TO SHAME. THEY'RE JUST SO HAPPY TO BE IN CHURCH.**
> —MEMBER
> *Buxmont Christian Church*

SHARING THE GOSPEL

By developing nurturing relationships in a fun and welcoming environment, Mike believes that he and his staff can communicate the love of God to the Pug Wugs. "We teach them about Jesus, we pray together, we teach a Bible story each week, we praise God—they all seem receptive to the gospel," he says. "They love to hear about Jesus."

Two of the Pug Wugs have become members of Buxmont Christian Church, and they and others often attend services there. "Sometimes six to eight developmentally challenged adults come to worship service on Sunday morning; sometimes all of the members of a whole group home [a supervised residential living arrangement] will come. And we have a few who come to Sunday school as well," he says.

In addition to the all-important goal of learning about Jesus, the Pug Wugs program is just plain fun for the participants. "We get lots of thank-you cards from the parents, telling us how great it is and how much the Pug Wugs love it," says Mike. "One parent told us that his son kept asking to go to Pugs, even though we were off for a holiday. They miss it when the program isn't in session."

CHAPTER FOURTEEN
IMPLEMENTATION

HOW YOUR CHURCH CAN REACH OUT TO DEVELOPMENTALLY CHALLENGED ADULTS

If the idea of reaching out in some way to developmentally challenged people appeals to you and your church, follow these simple principles:

Principle 1—Communicate—and receive—love generously.
Principle 2—Begin simply, allowing the ministry to grow naturally.
Principle 3—Don't be afraid to make changes along the way. Be adaptable.
Principle 4—Have fun!

STEPS TO TAKE

1. Poll your staff and congregation to gauge interest and identify possible participants. Use the pulpit and your church bulletin to outline your ideas, and monitor the response.
2. Decide what facilities and resources the church can offer. Room size is a major consideration. Ten to 12 in a room, plus staff, is the maximum in Mike's ministry, especially when doing crafts.

Rating Your Facility

Depending on your facility, you may need to add wheelchair ramps, wider doors, or other modifications to accommodate a special needs ministry. These specifications are probably already part of your local building code requirements, so if your building already meets Americans with Disabilities Act standards, you're set.

As a general guideline, if your building was constructed in the United States after 1990, it was probably designed with the ADA in mind. But even if you meet in an older facility, the amount of reconstruction required may depend on how your church is used. Religious organizations are exempt from the ADA's title III requirements for public accommodations, as long as the building is used only for worship.

If any other meetings take place in the building—such as community meetings, daycare, or other non-worship functions—the ADA requirements apply. If you have questions about your facility, call the ADA Information Line at 1-800-514-0301 or visit the ADA home page at www.ada.gov. Another good source of information that will help you welcome people with disabilities into your congregation is available from the National Organization on Disability. The Religion and Disability Program of NOD offers its updated seventh edition of That All May Worship: An Interfaith Welcome to People with Disabilities. *This guide offers common sense advice to religious organizations about becoming more accessible and welcoming to people with disabilities.*

According to NOD statistics, many barriers exist to prevent America's 54 million men, women, and children with disabilities from participating in worship and religious study. Some simple solutions, says Ginny Thornburgh, Director of NOD's Religion and Disability Program, include "improving lighting and sound systems, enlarging printed material, and providing transportation and assistance with heavy doors," as well as providing ramps and other structural accommodations.

3. Identify a staff member or someone in the congregation who has the passion and gifts to lead this ministry, and work with him or her to take the following steps:
   - Recruit a team of volunteers who want to reach out to developmentally challenged adults.
   - Consult with a special education professional. Your local high school or college would be a good source of information and advice. Explain the type of program and activities you wish to offer, and ask the specialist to review and comment on your plans. Also ask if the professional

would be willing to be "on call" if you have questions as you begin the program. (Be sure to send the specialist an invitation to your grand opening!) Convey your findings to your team.

- Choose a small team to develop your curriculum. Be prepared to revise existing material to fit the needs of your group.

Developing a Curriculum

There are a few basic ideas to keep in mind as you develop or adapt a curriculum for developmentally challenged adults. Pat Verbal, author, speaker, and founder of the Ministry to Today's Child in Frisco, Texas, offers this advice:

- One option is to start with a curriculum geared toward a first- or second-grade vocabulary and then add more mature-looking graphics. "You don't want to use something that looks like it came out of a children's coloring book," says Pat. "You can use pictures of youth or 20- to 25-year-olds and make [the curriculum] look 'with it.' "

- Another option, she says, is to start with an adult curriculum and then simplify the language.

- Don't always use a lot of paper, says Pat. Use overhead transparencies or PowerPoint presentations. "This population loves visuals."

- Identify the one truth you want to get across on a given day, and "repeat it again and again," Pat says. "Reinforce it with music. Repetition is the best thing. They won't get bored."

- When it comes to crafts, don't necessarily gravitate toward children's activities. "Consider working with plaster, ceramics, or weaving," says Pat. The key, she says, is working in steps and providing visuals. Pat illustrates each step on a large sheet of poster board for her class to follow.

- Developmentally challenged adults love to make things to carry, says Pat. "Little pouches or boxes or purses that they can fit in a pocket and pull out" are a big hit, she says. And if there's a Scripture verse on it, that's even better. "Even if they can't read it, you've told them the verse, and they can pull out the little pouch and remember the verse and talk about it."

- Gifts are also a popular part of her craft program. For example, says Pat, your group might make something for all of the grandmas in the congregation or something to give to a kindergarten class. "They love to give things away."

- Finally, don't forget to offer service opportunities as part of your ministry. Here again, it's important to break the projects into simple steps. Pat once had her class wash the toys in the nursery. The first week, the group visited the nursery, looked at the toys, and talked about their project. Then the next week they actually washed and dried the toys. Another time, her group washed the pastor's car. "They took so much care in the details, making it shine. They felt a lot of pride and talked about that project for months." Of course, she laughs, it's important to get the pastor's permission first!

- With your team, realistically decide the particulars of the program.
  - › How many times will you meet? Every week might be too much; if so, start with monthly meetings.
  - › Consider liability issues. To get started, take a look at the risk-management assessment on pages 143-144. Mike says his Pug Wug program hasn't faced any liability problems because he doesn't provide transportation to events. You'll probably want to preview your plans with your church's legal counsel.

Special Needs—Special Ministry *(Group Publishing, 2004) is a great resource for helping you establish a ministry geared to people with special needs, whether they're adults or children.*

- › Set a budget. What kind of startup money is available? Will you ask participants for donations? If so, how much? Will the church be able to contribute?
- › Consider the extra activities you might want to sponsor, and figure those costs into the budget. Local restaurants and theaters might be willing to offer discounts to your ministry.
- › Estimate the supplies you'll need. Then consider asking your congregation and local businesses for donations. Budget for the remaining supplies.

- Call local group homes, other churches, and social service agencies to let them know about your ministry. Invite them to set up an appointment to tour your facility and discuss your program.
- Prepare to be blessed! "The Pug Wugs love the program, and we love being with them," says Mike. "I love seeing the smiles on their faces."

"AND THE KING WILL TELL THEM, 'I ASSURE YOU, WHEN YOU DID IT TO ONE OF THE LEAST OF THESE MY BROTHERS AND SISTERS, YOU WERE DOING IT TO ME!'"
—MATTHEW 25:40, NLT

CHAPTER FIFTEEN

REACH OUT TO NURSING HOME RESIDENTS

One couple has developed a ministry just for nursing home residents and in the process has touched thousands of lives.

- ☑ SERVES A GROWING, OFTEN NEGLECTED, POPULATION
- ☑ BUILDS AUTHENTIC RELATIONSHIPS
- ☑ LEADS TO IN-DEPTH DISCUSSIONS ABOUT FAITH
- ☑ CAN BE DONE BY ANY SIZE CHURCH OR GROUP

THE EVOLUTION OF THE IDEA

Buck Stanley became a Christian in 1987. A few years later, he and his wife, Clarice, were invited to visit a nursing home to sing and minister to the residents. Using a small, $85 keyboard, Buck sang and played for the seniors, assuring them that Jesus loved them and that they were precious in his eyes.

During that visit, Buck observed a woman whose nose and eye were ravaged by cancer. "The Lord put it on my heart to go and give her a kiss," Buck remembers. "But I argued with him. I didn't want to do it." Finally Buck obeyed, and an amazing thing happened. He saw a twinkle in her eye as she responded to this expression of God's love. And from that moment on, Buck was hooked.

He eventually left his job with a Florida power company to attend to his nursing home ministry full time. He and Clarice bought a motor home and set out, armed with little more than a boombox, a few instruments, and hearts set on serving God.

THE HEART OF THE MINISTRY

Steeped in old, bluegrass gospel music, Buck and Clarice traveled from nursing home to nursing home, singing for and with the residents and spreading the gospel. Then Buck decided to start a church to further their outreach.

The church began with a little building at the intersection of two busy highways in Grandin, Florida, and an old bus that had been used to transport migrant farmworkers. Instead of just visiting nursing homes, Buck began driving to the homes, picking up interested residents, and taking them to his little church for services every Sunday afternoon.

"Buck saw a need for someone to go get those residents," explains Nikki Schaub, who married Buck in 1994 after Clarice's death. "Some of them felt trapped, especially the people in wheelchairs. They felt like prisoners. Buck wanted to help them change environments for a while."

> "You know that movie, *The Apostle*, where the preacher goes out in the bus and brings people to his little church? That's Buck, only he brings people in wheelchairs. He's so on fire for Jesus!"
> —Nikki Stanley
> *Jacksonville, Florida*

Sometimes churches would drive their members from the nursing homes to the church, but they usually didn't include people in wheelchairs. "Buck fixed up that bus, added a lift, and went out and got those people," says Nikki. "He was willing to step out in faith and do something radical. The rest of us just followed along, waiting to see what Buck would do next," she laughs. The bus could accommodate 12 to 16 people, depending on their needs.

THE MINISTRY GROWS

In 1994, Nikki and Buck bought a bus that could accommodate more wheelchairs and residents. The couple ministered to nursing home residents at the nursing homes during the week (their "road ministry") and brought the residents to their church on Sundays (their "bus ministry"). "At one time," Nikki says, "about 75 nursing homes were part of our road ministry. Most of them were in Florida, but some were in North Carolina as well." Of course, Nikki and Buck couldn't visit them all in a week, so they developed a rotating schedule.

Sometimes they approached the nursing homes' activity directors and requested permission to deliver services to the residents. Other times, activity directors who had heard of the ministry called them directly and asked them to come.

Today the ministry calls Jacksonville, Florida, its home. "We don't live in a motor home anymore," says Nikki. "We have a little house, and we built a little 60x40-foot church behind the house. To accommodate wheelchairs, it has no pews and a tile floor."

> "We've worn out a few motor homes and trailers since those early days. We've gone from a boombox to sound systems."
> —Nikki Stanley

The ministry now has four buses that deliver 50 to 60 nursing home residents to Sunday services each week. During the week, Nikki and Buck continue their road ministry. Nikki estimates that they reach about 1,000 people each month.

The ministry also offers nursing home residents a newsletter, which is also featured on a weekly radio show in North Carolina.

SHARING THE GOSPEL

"The more I got involved," says Nikki, "the more I could see the ministry changing lives."

One woman, for example, regularly attended the church service. "She came every week, but she was hostile and angry—very hurt. She never talked. She might even scratch you if you tried to hug her.

"But we just kept loving her and bringing her to church each week. One Sunday I got on the bus and sat next to her. I put my arm around her as we rode. The trip was 23 miles each way. As we passed an open field, she pointed and said, 'Cows!' Somehow just being outside, with people who accepted her, broke her hardened exterior." From that time on, Nikki says, the woman became open, loving, and full of joy. "She just needed someone to show her God's love."

Recently, Nikki says, a woman in their ministry became a Christian. "She had attended our services for years; she loved attending. After hearing the gospel again and again, she finally made a faith commitment." This particular woman, says Nikki, had had a stroke, which had made speaking particularly difficult and laborious. "We've learned to be patient, continually showing the true love of Jesus."

And it's not only the residents who are touched by the gospel. Sometimes members of the administrative staff listen to the services, and sometimes nurses or aides are in the room during services. "Some staff members have made a faith commitment. Others have said they had strayed from their faith and have realized their need to return."

> **THERE'S SUCH A HARVEST. MORE AND MORE NURSING HOMES ARE BEING BUILT. WE'LL ALL BE LIVING IN ONE BEFORE YOU KNOW IT!**
> —NIKKI STANLEY

FUNDING THE MINISTRY

Funding for the ministry has come in several forms over the years. But the source is always the same, declares Nikki. "There's one source, and that source isn't man. It's God. God always provides."

In the beginning, Buck used his own savings to fund the ministry. Today, in addition to personal resources, money for the ministry comes from four avenues:

1. **Nursing homes.** "Sometimes the nursing homes' activity directors use money from their entertainment budgets to pay us," Nikki explains. But that didn't happen overnight.

"You've got to pave the way," says Buck. "You have to prove yourself and show that the residents need and want what you have to offer. A workman has to be worthy of his hire."

2. **Family donations.** "Sometimes family members of the residents donate money; some even make monthly contributions," says Nikki. "They appreciate what we do for the residents."

3. **Missionary offerings.** Since the ministry is nondenominational, it doesn't benefit from a denomination's mission support. Still, several churches have adopted Nikki and Buck as "home missionaries." For example, says Nikki, one Baptist church in North Carolina has called the workers in this ministry its missionaries for 13 years.

4. **Random donations.** Nikki has many stories about individuals who have contributed to the cause. "Sometimes we'll be driving along, and people in another car will motion us to pull over. They tell us they read our sign on the motor home saying this is a nursing home ministry, and they want to encourage us. Then they'll hand us a $50 bill," says Nikki. Or someone in a gas station will offer to fill the tank.

"One time, out of the blue, a doctor's wife called and said she wanted to donate money to the ministry," recalls Nikki. "She'd been in one of the nursing homes during our service. We didn't think about it too much, but the next week we got a check for $4,000!"

Then there's the owner of a campground who lets Nikki and Buck stay there for free, fills their tank, and gives them free propane when they show up during their travels. "He's also given us cash donations," Nikki says. "He even feeds us!

"It's like Elijah being fed by the ravens. Everywhere we go, we're taken care of. It's an exciting adventure."

Other support comes in the form of gifts for the nursing home residents. "People give us stuffed animals and other tokens of love to give to the residents," Nikki says. "The residents keep them in their rooms as reminders that we love them and that we're praying for them. Those little gifts encourage them and help them deal with pain and lonely nights."

> **We want them to know that the Lord's with them through it all. We encourage them to run the race to the end and cross those wheelchairs over the finish line.**
> —Nikki Stanley

RIPPLE EFFECTS

One of the great joys of their nursing home outreach, says Nikki, is seeing how it strengthens the residents. "They return to the nursing homes encouraged and renewed," she says. "And they become lights to the people there."

Nikki and Buck encourage the residents to be prayer warriors in their facilities. "We encourage them to be content where they are and to find peace and joy in God. God has a purpose, and he's coming back for them. In the meantime, they can pray for their nurses and aides. They can pray for other residents. They can forgive past hurts and find rest in God's love."

And according to Nikki, some of the greatest blessings come *to* the ministry, not from it. "We receive more than we give," she says. "We see the faith of these people, and we're blessed and strengthened ourselves."

> ❝YOU'RE NEVER TOO OLD OR WEAK TO BE STRONG IN THE BODY OF CHRIST.❞
> —NIKKI STANLEY

The ministry has also helped Nikki and Buck face the future. "We're not afraid of what lies ahead of us," declares Nikki. "We see the joy possible in a nursing home, so if God places us there one day, we'll just view it as a mission field."

LESSONS LEARNED

As this ministry has developed and grown, Nikki and Buck have learned many lessons. But the most important lesson they've learned is a valuable reminder to all Christians contemplating how to serve and bless others—to trust the Lord. "Walk with the Lord," says Nikki. "That's all that matters. Just be faithful day by day, and you'll see great and wonderful things."

I M P L E M E N T A T I O N

HOW YOUR CHURCH CAN REACH OUT TO NURSING HOME RESIDENTS

I f two people with a heart for nursing home residents can reach 1,000 people a month, imagine what your church could do if it were committed to this neglected—and growing—segment of the population! If this idea resonates with you and your church, remember these principles as you develop your own outreach:

Principle 1—Do what's necessary to develop meaningful relationships with nursing home residents. Many have shut down emotionally because few, if any, of their past relationships exist and no one has invested the time or energy to get to know them. Look beyond vacant stares to the person within.

Principle 2—Recognize the riches many of these people possess. Their experiences, their values, their perspectives can be invaluable to younger people, whether they're children, teenagers, adults just starting careers and families, or middle-aged people.

Principle 3—As much as possible, enable the residents to leave the nursing home temporarily in order to experience new surroundings.

Principle 4—Recognize how important anticipation is in everyone's life, especially those with unvarying routines. Without something to look forward to, it's easy to become discouraged and apathetic.

Principle 5—Find ways to integrate nursing home residents into the life of your church.

STEPS TO TAKE

1. Spend time in prayer to discern whether God is calling your church to this type of ministry.

2. Talk to the people in your congregation who have a special compassion and affinity for the aged, and identify ways your church can reach out to them.

3. Decide how far-reaching you want your ministry to be. If yours is a small church, you might want to begin by adopting the residents of the nursing home nearest to your facility. A larger church might decide to minister to the residents of nursing homes within a 10-mile radius of the church.

4. Meet with the activity directors of the nursing homes you hope to reach. Find out what the most pressing needs are and how your church might best serve and honor the residents.

5. If you decide to take your ministry to the nursing homes, determine what type of service you want to provide. While Nikki and Buck don't deliver the same service in each nursing home, they do follow a general outline: lots of music, a gospel message, and Scripture reading. "We read from the Bible so the residents hear the Word of God. We tell them the good news about Jesus. And they love to sing the old songs they remember."

   Favorites, says Nikki, are hymns such as "The Old Rugged Cross" and "In the Garden." But they usually start with a few upbeat, joyful songs to get those toes tapping. Nikki and Buck provide background music soundtracks on their Web site for other churches to use (www.nikkiandbuck.com).

6. Consider offering audiotapes of each service. "We bought a duplicator," Nikki says, "and right after the service, I make tapes to hand out. I've been told that the residents listen to them until the tapes are worn out."

7. Identify plenty of ways for the members of your church to interact with the nursing home residents. Be sure to vary venues for your get-togethers so that the residents are stimulated and have things to look forward to. Consider intergenerational Bible studies and small groups, coffees at church before or after the service, and celebrations to mark significant events in the nursing home residents' lives.

> **WE'VE GOT IT DOWN TO A SCIENCE NOW. WE HAVE ALL OUR MUSICAL EQUIPMENT ON CARTS SO WE CAN JUST WHEEL THEM IN AND GET STARTED. IN FOUR MINUTES, WE CAN BE PLUGGED IN, SET UP, AND SINGING.**
> —NIKKI STANLEY

FINAL THOUGHTS ON...GIVING UP

Nikki urges anyone embarking on a ministry to nursing home residents not to become discouraged. "Sometimes the residents won't seem to be alert. They won't respond. Don't let that prevent you from returning," Nikki cautions. "Look beyond it."

After the service, she advises, talk to the residents. Sometimes even if their eyes are closed, they're wide awake. "One time after a service I went up to a resident who I thought had been sleeping the whole time. She opened her eyes and smiled, saying, 'I really needed this.'

"Don't ever doubt the Holy Spirit's ability to reach these precious people."

> "SO NOW I AM GIVING YOU A NEW COMMANDMENT: LOVE EACH OTHER. JUST AS I HAVE LOVED YOU, YOU SHOULD LOVE EACH OTHER."
> —JOHN 13:34, NLT

NOTES

NOTES